USEFUL WORKSHOP TOOLS

Stan Bray

T0347310

SPECIAL INTEREST MODEL BOOKS

Special Interest Model Books Ltd.
P.O Box 327
Poole
Dorset
BH15 2RG
England
www.specialinterestmodelbooks.co.uk

First published by Nexus Special Interests, 2000
This edition published by Special Interest Model Books, 2008
Reprinted 2012, 2015, 2017, 2018
© Stan Bray 2000

ISBN 978 1 85486 194 8

Printed and bound in Malta by Melita Press

Contents

A Micrometer Stand

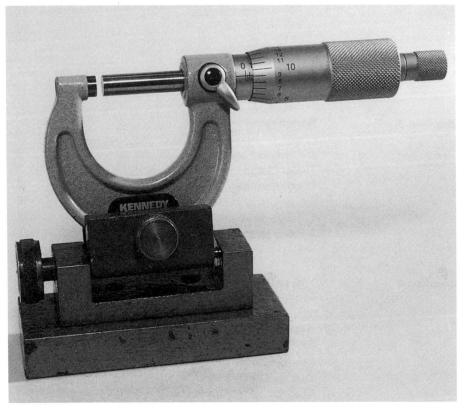

The photograph demonstrates clearly how the micrometer sits in the stand. The angle for reading is adjusted via the screw on the left

A micrometer stand is a very useful piece of equipment, although no doubt many people will be asking themselves why on earth we should want such a thing. It has two functions, firstly it enables work to be measured without having to juggle the micrometer on the palm of the hand in order to adjust it, while the other hand holds the work. Doing this means fiddling about with ones fingers in order to adjust the micrometer thimble for reading, while trying to hold it in the same hand.

Using a stand allows the hand to be used solely for adjustment while the other one can grip the work quite firmly. This in turn prevents little errors creeping in as they can if for any reason the work should twist as it is located between the jaws. It also means

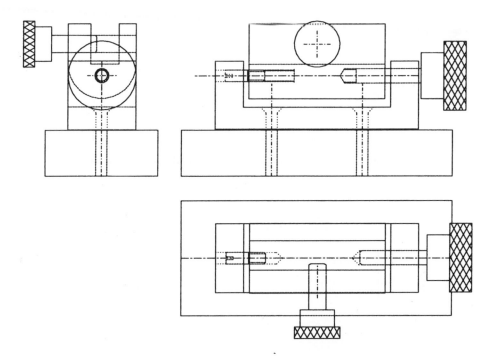

General Arrangement Drawing of Micrometer Stand

that micrometers are not left lying around on the bench where they can suffer damage from knocks and dirt. It is a good idea to put the assembly on a low shelf at the back of the bench, bringing the micrometer to a nice readable height. Rather than having to bend ones knees to see it. But should it have to be located down on the bench, it is still easy to read, thanks to the swivelling action.

The construction of the stand is simplicity in itself and the drawings are more or less self-explanatory. The whole thing is made of mild steel, except the screw that secures the micrometer in the stand which should be either brass or plastic to avoid damage to the instrument.

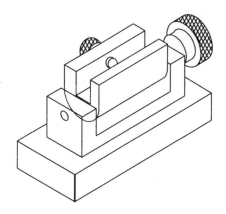

An isometric drawing of the swivelling micrometer stand as seen from the opposite side to that shown in the photograph.

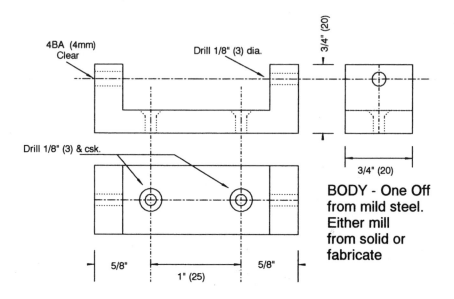

4BA (4mm) Clear

Drill 1/8" (3) dia.

3/4" (20)

3/4" (20)

Drill 1/8" (3) & csk.

5/8"

1" (25)

5/8"

BODY - One Off from mild steel. Either mill from solid or fabricate

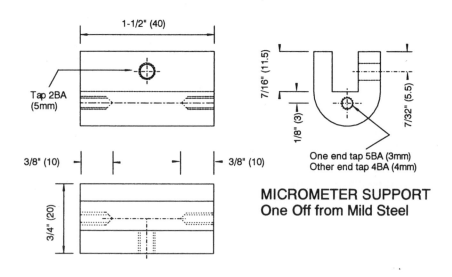

1-1/2" (40)

Tap 2BA (5mm)

3/8" (10)

3/8" (10)

3/4" (20)

7/16" (11.5)

1/8" (3)

7/32" (5.5)

One end tap 5BA (3mm)
Other end tap 4BA (4mm)

MICROMETER SUPPORT
One Off from Mild Steel

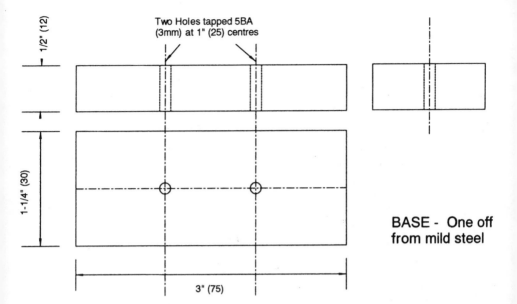

Two Holes tapped 5BA (3mm) at 1" (25) centres

1/2" (12)

1-1/4" (30)

3" (75)

BASE - One off from mild steel

The Body

It is probably as well to start by making the body and there are two ways of doing this. It can either be machined from a solid piece, or three pieces of flat stock can be used and the two ends screwed in position using either countersunk or hexagon cap screws. The heads of which should be recessed. There is a hole at either end to accept the screws that act as swivel and locking pins and these should be drilled using the four-jaw chuck on the lathe. If the body is fabricated the holes can be made before assembly which makes life easy. If it is from a single piece then obviously the slot should be milled first. The countersunk holes for securing the body to the base are straightforward enough and the drilling machine can be used for them.

The parts could be clamped together for drilling, but it might be easier to use an adhesive to hold them

The Base

The base is a plain piece of flat stock, with two tapped holes to accept the screws that secure the body to it. To get them exactly right calls for either perfect marking out or the use of co-ordinates if a. mill drill is available. The third way and one that can be recommended to the novice, particularly if he or she does not have access to a mill drill, is to stick them together and pass the drill through the top component. The best material to hold parts like this together is double-sided adhesive tape particularly the variety sold in DIY shops for sticking down carpets. An alternative would be to use a cyano-

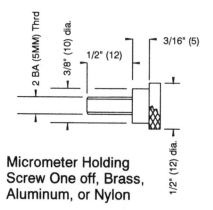

Micrometer Holding Screw One off, Brass, Aluminum, or Nylon

be vulnerable to rust and any enamel will do, as will one of the modern acrylics. If for any reason you would prefer not to paint it a rust proof finish can be obtained by other means. Simply heat the parts until they are a dull red colour and then brush oil over them. Any type of oil will do and it can be a good use for old sump oil. It is a job best done in the open air as a lot of smelly black smoke is created. The end result will be a matt black finish which is pleasing to the eye, professional looking and rust proof.

acrylic adhesive (Super Glue) It needs one with a high viscocity. The parts can be separated afterwards by giving one a sharp tap with a soft hammer.

Micrometer Support

The micrometer support is also very easy, two holes are needed in the ends that locate with those in the end supports and once again should be drilled and tapped in the lathe to ensure they are square. A slot is milled to accept the micrometer and a hole cross drilled and tapped for the securing screw and that is all there is to it. Note the ends are tapped different sizes and the slot is not central. Round off the botom with a file.

Screws

The three screws are ordinary turning jobs, the pivot screw having to be slotted for adjustments to be made. The other two should be machined and threaded, knurled and then parted off from solid bar
Finishing
It is worth applying a coat of paint to this particular device otherwise it will

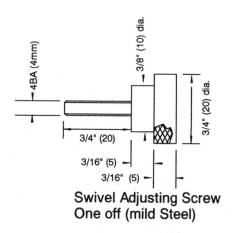

Swivel Adjusting Screw One off (mild Steel)

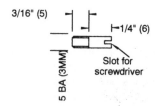

Swivel Screw One Off- Mild Steel

Finger Plates

Two views of a more or less standard type of finger plate. It differs from the drawings in as much as the holes used for working on screws and similar items are placed in a circular array, The drawings show them in a straight line. There is no hard and fast rule, they should be placed wherever they are needed for the work to be done.

Finger plates are usually associated with watch and clock making but they are extremely useful for all sorts of model engineering purposes. There is nothing complicated about them as they are simply a form of clamp and yet are very expensive to buy. They can easily be made from any scrap material that is around the workshop and have the beauty of being completely adaptable to the work in hand.

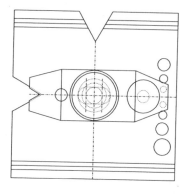

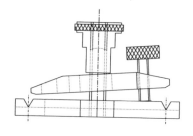

The drawing shows a more or less standard type, while the photographs show several minor variations.

The Base

The base is made from a piece of flat steel, in theory it should be hardened and ground and so ideally a piece of gauge plate is the best material to use. The reason for hardening is purely to prevent wear from files and other tools and the grinding is obviously carried out to get a good accurate flat surface. In general neither of the attributes are required for normal workshop use and so an ordinary piece of flat mild steel

A selection of finger plates of varying shapes and designs, which have generally been made for a particular job.

8

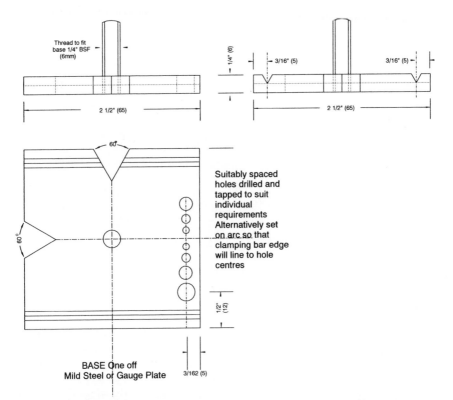

Thread to fit base 1/4" BSF (6mm)

1/4" (6)

3/16" (5)

3/16" (5)

2 1/2" (65)

2 1/2" (65)

60°

60°

Suitably spaced holes drilled and tapped to suit individual requirements
Alternatively set on arc so that clamping bar edge will line to hole centres

1/2" (12)

BASE One off
Mild Steel or Gauge Plate

3/162 (5)

plate will do the job just as well and if it is to be used for excessive work it can be case hardened. The drawing shows what is generally required to make the base, a hole in the centre and then various grooves, cut outs and holes, we will deal shortly with these, which obviously must be made at an early stage if hardening is to take place. The hole in the centre takes the pillar that the clamp floats about on and it is essential that it is square to the base. To make sure of this, it is probably as well to drill and tap it in the four-jaw chuck of the lathe. The pil-

lar is a length of studding and it is quite satisfactory to secure it with retaining compound although originally a force fit would have been used.

The various grooves have their purposes which in general are self explanatory, the long one is for holding round bars, the vee to allow for drilling, etc. and the holes are drilled and tapped, or left as clearance sizes as desired for working on screwed material. A personal preference is to make these in semi-circular form as it is then easier to swing the clamping bar over them. If the plate is not to be

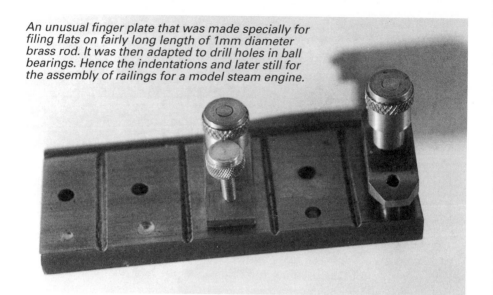

An unusual finger plate that was made specially for filing flats on fairly long length of 1mm diameter brass rod. It was then adapted to drill holes in ball bearings. Hence the indentations and later still for the assembly of railings for a model steam engine.

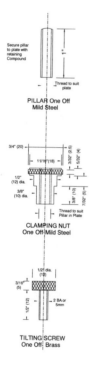

Secure pillar to plate with retaining Compound

1"

Thread to suit plate

PILLAR One Off
Mild Steel

3/4" (20)

3/32" (2.5)
5/32" (4)

11/16"(18)

1/2" (12) dia.

3/8" (10) dia.

3/8" (10)
7/32" (5)

Thread to suit
Pillar in Plate

CLAMPING NUT
One Off Mild Steel

1/2" dia.
(12)

3/16" (5)

1/2" (12)

2 BA or 5mm

TILTING SCREW
One Off Brass

hardened make the minimum number of cut outs and holes and put them in as and when required. Apart from appearance there is no reason why the holes should be evenly spaced it being better to place them at the points where they will be most convenient to work with. For example if a short length of round stock needs work carried out at each end. Make the vee groove across a corner and when clamped down each end will be available.

Clamping Bar

Again nothing very complicated simply a suitable bar generally of mild steel with a groove in the centre and a drilled and tapped hole at either end. Angles are machined on the top to allow easier access to work and a

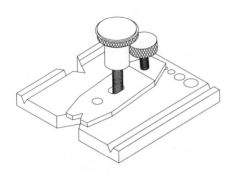

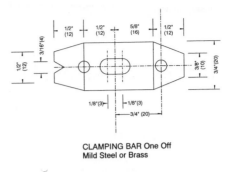

CLAMPING BAR One Off
Mild Steel or Brass

small vee can also be of help. It may be best to make the vee in one end and leave the other plain and also make the angles slightly different to allow for different types of work. As the bar will be clamped at an angle a small section can be machined off the bottom at each end, otherwise if left at ninety degrees much of the clamping power is lost. It is not of course possible to get the angles at the bottom to exactly match the work in hand but any shallow angle will have a better effect than the square corners. These angles must be flat and so they should not be filed. It has been known for the bottom angle to be replaced with another small groove, where the finger plate was to be used purely for round bar work. If possible make the bar reversible for even greater flexibility. If soft material such as brass is to be worked on make the clamping bar from brass so as not to mark the work and if the work is of a particularly sensitive nature it can be from a hard plastic material.

Clamping Nut

Simply a piece of mild steel bar, drilled and tapped in the lathe, a section machined to a smaller diameter and then the larger diameter knurled. We also require a lifting screw to get the clamping angle and this is specified as brass to avoid marking the base plate, although if that is hardened there is no reason why the screw should not be steel. Both these parts need to be sympathetic towards each other, the clamping bar will be moved to different positions on the pillar and it is essential that the lifting screw will fit underneath the knurled section otherwise it will become impossible to make adjustments.

There we have it, a simple little device with many uses and easy enough to make for any particular job and the ideal way to use up some of that scrap material that has been hanging around for the last ten years, because sometime it will come in useful.

Depth Gauges

Variations on a theme. On the left a standard depth gauge made to the drawings shown at the end of the chapter. On the right is a spring loaded gauge, made half-size for a special job.

Making a depth gauge is a favourite exercise that used to be given to school children in the old days of metal work classes. At times there were some weird and wonderful end results and it is doubtful anyway whether ninety percent of the pupils really grasped the value of the tool. Yet at least one should find its place in every workshop as it is invaluable when setting work in a vice, or measuring the depth of holes or checking the length of a cut on the lathe. In fact

uses for it can be found in all sorts of situations.

The manufacture of the gauge hardly required a description as the drawings are self explanatory. It consist of three parts, a base or body, a probe or pin and a screw. The body is simply a piece of metal bar with a hole drilled right through the centre and another cross drilled and tapped For the sake of appearance if one wishes the ends of the bar can be rounded off, which also protects the user from possibly

USEFUL WORKSHOP TOOLS

A standard type depth gauge being use to check the height of a casting above the machine vice jaws

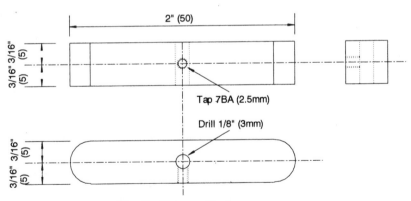

2" (50)

3/16" 3/16"
(5)

Tap 7BA (2.5mm)

Drill 1/8" (3mm)

3/16" 3/16"
(5)

Depth Gauge Body
This version differs from the general arrangement as the ends are rounded.

cutting themselves on any sharp edges that might be there.

The probe is a piece of thin round bar and in fact needs to be nothing more. It is an advantage to use silver steel because of its better wearing properties but it can be of mild steel if one so wishes. The drawings show a probe with a top on. It is not unknown for a depth gauge probe to slide right through the body when the screw is undone and disappear. We all know what that means, it will not be found until a new one has been made. By fitting a top this is prevented. If a top is being made it might at as well be a nice one and could be of brass or steel. Knurling it will make it easier to use. It can be screwed directly on to the probe.

One thing that is advisable is to make a small flat along the length of the probe, for the screw to lock on to.

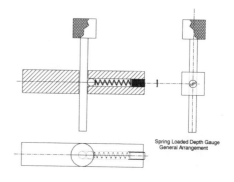

Spring Loaded Depth Gauge
General Arrangement

In the sizes we are talking about there is virtually no surface area whatever on the circumference of the probe and it will be very difficult to keep it in place no matter how much the screw is tightened up. The flat can be milled or filed and the finger plate provides an excellent means of holding it while it is dealt with.

The retaining screw can also be of either brass or steel, brass will of course be less likely to damage the probe if the latter is made from mild steel. The head of the screw should be knurled to assist one in getting a good grip and for the same reason should be of as large a diameter as practical. Normally the size will be limited by the size of the body as if the screw is a larger diameter than the depth of that, it will foul on the work and the gauge will not settle flat when in use. It is possible to make a series of marks at known intervals along the probe, as a

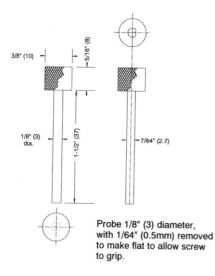

Probe 1/8" (3) diameter, with 1/64" (0.5mm) removed to make flat to allow screw to grip.

USEFUL WORKSHOP TOOLS

guide to what depth it will be set at. If this is done then obviously great care must be taken to ensure accuracy.

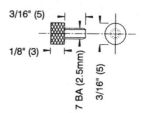

Depth Gauge Adjuster Screw

Spring Loaded Gauge

The type of depth gauge described above have been in use for many years with every success. There are situation where even such a simple tool can be difficult to use. Here is an example of a depth gauge that can be operated with one hand and is such a delight to use that many will be tempted to use it all the time, rather than the more conventional type.

It is very similar to the normal type of gauge and for this reason only a general arrangement drawing is given. The probe is virtually identical, but no flat along its length will be needed. Pressure will be applied using a ball bearing instead of a screw. Of course a ball bearing can be set in the more conventional gauge, except the posi-

tion of the screw leaves little if any room to fit one. In the spring loaded model the screw hole is set at the end of the body and passes right through to the hole for the probe. The ball bearing, the diameter of which should be just a little less that the hole diameter is kept in place by the spring from a ball point pen. This in turn is tensioned by a grub screw. In use the probe is simply slid up and down and providing the spring has been properly tensioned will stay in position.

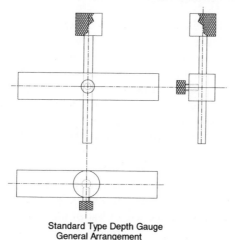

Standard Type Depth Gauge
General Arrangement

Finger Clamps

An example of a finger clamp. The body of this one has been fabricated from flat steel strip as explained in the text.

Finger Clamps are not to be confused with finger plates, which we will come to later. The clamp is so described only because the clamping section has the appearance of a finger. They are used in conjunction with a drilling machine as a rule and are very quick in operation, which means they can be particularly effective when there are a number of similarly positioned holes to be drilled. With the clamp bolted firmly to the table it requires only a couple of turns of the wheel to hold the work firmly in position

The Body

The obvious place to start is with the body and there are a couple of ways in which this can be made. It can be milled from a solid steel block, or as suggested fabricated from three pieces. It could even be broken down further than this if need be.

The bottom part is a plain piece of steel stock of suitable size with a slot milled in it to allow it to be clamped to the drilling table. The ends are pieces of bar of the same size and each has a recess milled or filed in it to accommodate the other parts of the tool. Anyone who has not got milling recourses should not be put off as it is not all that difficult, or perhaps more importantly, too much hard work for the recesses to be sawn and filed. No doubt most readers will be familiar with the technique known as chain drilling, where a series of closely spaced holes are drilled along a line allowing the unwanted piece of metal to be broken off. The idea can be used in this case, the only problem being that it is essential that the holes are drilled in such a way that they break into each other. It is best therefore if this method is chosen to use progressively larger drills to make the holes, and as long as sufficient accuracy has been achieved there will be no problem.

Achieving such accuracy is not always as easy as it sounds and whilst it does not matter too much if things go a little wrong on thin sheet problems arise when using thick bar as in this case. If therefore one is not confi-

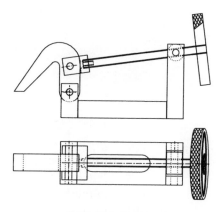

General Arrangement
of finger clamp

**BODY - Mild Steel.
Make from three
pieces. Join with
4mm (4BA) cap
screws**

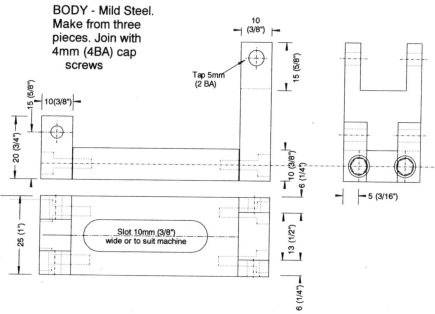

In order to use any available material, as long as proportions are kept reasonably the same, the actual size of the clamp can be varied to suit individual requirements. Here we see two clamps of different sizes

dent on being able to mark out sufficiently accurately to get the chain drilling right, a hack saw and file method can be used. Start by sawing the two vertical cuts virtually to full depth. Next make a cut diagonally from the top of one of these to the bottom of the other. A nice triangle will now fall out. About half way along the angle that is left cut another angular piece in the opposite direction, aiming for the bottom of the second vertical cut. We are now left with an apex, make a diagonal cut again from half way up this and repeat on the other side, which should leave very little metal at the bottom of the recess to be filed flat.

Drill all the required holes but those for the screws that will hold the parts together, just make tapping size

at present. Deburr them all and then the screw holes must be transferred to the base. This can be done with careful marking out or alternatively they can be spotted through from the ends. To do this stick the parts together temporarily using either a suitable cyanoacrylic adhesive, or double sided tape. Finally after tapping all the necessary holes, open out the screw holes in the ends to clearance size and counterbore them to allow the specified cap screw heads to recess into them. These screws have been specified because of their additional strength but good quality countersunk screws would probably do the job.

The Nose

There is nothing very difficult about this part of the clamp even though at

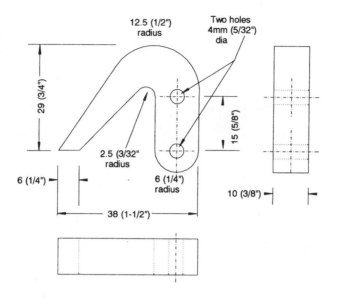

NOSE, Mild Steel

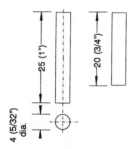

NOSE PINS
Two types both
from Bronze

first glance it may appear complicated. The radii that are given are not critical so don't spend too much time trying to get then right.

Nose Pivot
Here we are back again to a similar situation that arose with the ends of the base, a hefty piece of metal to be removed. The hole for the pin should be drilled before any metal is cut away and should be done in the lathe to ensure it is square. Two pins are needed one being shorter to pass through the pivot and nose and a longer one to

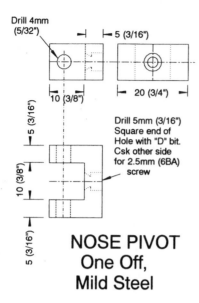

NOSE PIVOT
One Off,
Mild Steel

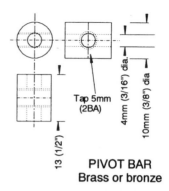

PIVOT BAR
Brass or bronze

go through the body and pivot.

Adjusting Wheel

The wheel can be of any reasonable diameter in order to use available material but have in mind that it needs to apply a certain amount of torque, which will be difficult, if it is too small. The recess is purely for show and need not be machined in, unless one so wishes, the knurl though is needed in order to get a decent grip. It is held to the screw with a lock nut, which has been found to be a perfectly satisfactory arrangement but a square on the end of the screw and in the wheel, would be a more professional way of doing things.

The screw was made from an odd length of studding. If it has to be threaded then there is no point whatever in doing so over the full length,

sufficient to allow the clamp to tighten is all that will be needed. The end that fits the nose pivot is smooth to allow it to rotate easily and that end is also drilled and tapped for the countersunk screw that holds the screw to the nose pivot.

Pivot Bar

A piece of bronze bar was used for the pivot in order to allow for wear, but brass will do. It sits on the two pivot screws that in turn are fitted in the body and is threaded for the clamping screw. The pivot screws should be

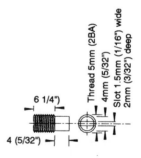

Pivot Screws
two Off
Mild Steel

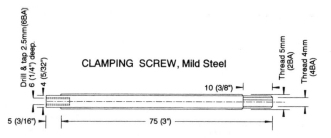

CLAMPING SCREW, Mild Steel

Drill & tap 2.5mm(6BA)
6 (1/4") deep.
4 (5/32")
5 (3/16")
75 (3")
10 (3/8")
Thread 5mm (2BA)
Thread 4mm (4BA)

tightened in such a way that the bar can swing freely on them.

Alternative Construction

Not everyone will have suitable material to hand to make tools of this nature. The material used for the base for example may be a little on the thick side to be found in many home workshops. The component could be fabricated with care from square stock, using two lengths for the bottom, bolted together with spacers. The base uprights could also be from similar material, using pieces with the ends machined square in the four jaw chuck of the lathe, and again screwing in spacers. The wheel also could be made from lengths of flat stock in the form of a cross, rather on

the lines of a capstan handle, there are all sorts of possibilities.

Further Uses

Although designed basically for use on the drilling machine it will be found that the clamp has uses elsewhere. A particularly useful aspect is the fact that they can be bolted to angle plates to hold work that is in the vertical position. A pair of them screwed to a bench are perfect for holding long lengths of plate firmly in position for marking out. If the nose is made of a soft material they are ideal for holding clock wheels for polishing, the quick release action speeding up considerably the number of wheels that can be dealt with in a given period of time.

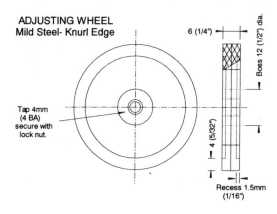

ADJUSTING WHEEL
Mild Steel- Knurl Edge

6 (1/4")
Boss 12 (1/2") dia.

Tap 4mm (4 BA) secure with lock nut.

4 (5/32")

Recess 1.5mm (1/16")

Cross Drilling Jigs

The Vee Block

A typical vee block type of cross drilling jig. Comparitively easy to make, it relies on the accuracy of the hole in relationship to the bottom of the vee.
Different plates can be made to fit the same block and a row of holes can also be produced.

One of the most awkward jobs we need to do in model engineering is to drill centrally across the diameter of a round bar., without some sort of aid. It all seems so simple look along the length of the bar, line up the drill and away we go, but rarely does it happen like that. The tiniest fraction off centre and the drill moves sideways and continues drilling at an angle Fortunately there are a number of gadgets which will help us to get things a little more accurate. They range from simple ideas to some quite complicated machine tools. The idea of this book is to make things as simple as possible and so only the easy ideas will be dealt with.

The Cross Bar

This idea for which no tool construction is needed, works quite well on large diameter material but is not very successful on smaller work. Even so it has its place, even if only because the tools that will be described are basically for smaller work and although larger versions can be made they are not too practical. The cross bar system requires either a short ruler or short length of thin flat bar. It is laid across the work at ninety degrees as near to central as is practical by eye. The point of a drill or centre drill is lowered on to the rule or metal strip, which will tip at an angle if the drill does not line up exactly centrally on the work. It becomes a case of trial and error to get the bar to stay level and when it does the drill is lined up exactly centrally to the round bar. Obviously the system is open to some slight errors as we are relying on the human eye to tell us whether or not the crosspiece is exact-

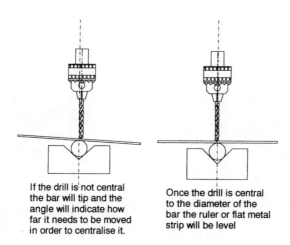

If the drill is not central the bar will tip and the angle will indicate how far it needs to be moved in order to centralise it.

Once the drill is central to the diameter of the bar the ruler or flat metal strip will be level

Using a small ruler or thin steel strip to line up a round bar for cross drilling

ly level. Results though can be remarkably accurate and the idea is certainly well worth while using where larger diameter work is concerned. It will also work equally as well when trying to get a milling cutter lined up centrally over a round section.

Substitution
Again the method does not need any tool to be made and it will work on any sized round section of or below the maximum opening of a drill chuck. A piece of round bar of the same diameter as the work to be cross drilled is put in the drill chuck, which is then lowered so that the edge touches the fixed jaw of a machine vice. The vice is then bolted to the machine, while still in contact with the round section. Making sure that when tightened down it remains in contact. Any work of that diameter will, when placed in the vice be exactly centrally situated under the centre of the drill chuck.

The Vee Block
This is probably the most popular tool for cross drilling and needs little description. A simple vee block is needed, and while one can be purchased it is better to make one for oneself as that way it is easier to get the size required.

Making a vee block is not all that

Two Bar Method

A very simple device that is easily made to fit any size on metal. Works equally well with, round, flat or square metal and can be used for spaced holes if required Note use of cap head screws as pivots.

The substitution method of cross drilling requires nothing more than a length of bar of the same diameter as that which is to be drilled.

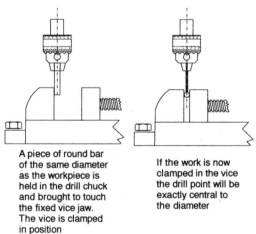

A piece of round bar of the same diameter as the workpiece is held in the drill chuck and brought to touch the fixed vice jaw. The vice is clamped in position

If the work is now clamped in the vice the drill point will be exactly central to the diameter

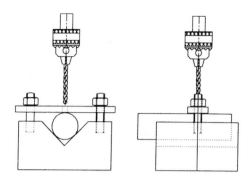

Diagram showing construction of vee block type of cross drilling jig, Sizes will depend entirely on the work it is to be used for, It does have the advantage that suitable jigs can be made for very large diameter work.

difficult, simply set a square bar, across the milling vice at an angle and then pass an end mill along it until the required depth of vee is obtained. The angle of the vee is not too important and while forty five degrees is possibly the most desirable setting a few degrees either way will be of no consequence.

Once the vee block is made, take a piece of flat plate and drill three holes in it, in line with each other, make sure they are thoroughly deburred. Line the central hole with the centre of the vee by pushing through a length of steel rod that has a point on it. When satisfied that the hole is lined up stick the bar at exactly ninety degrees across the vee, using double sided adhesive tape. The outer holes can now be transferred to the vee block. Those on the bar will need afterwards to be opened out to the clearance size of

whatever thread has been chosen to screw the parts together, while those in the vee block are tapped accordingly.

If round bar is laid along the vee then the centre hole of the crosspiece will be exactly above the centre of it. Before using it pass a drill through and into the vee to make a relief hole and it might be worth opening this the tiniest fraction to allow free movement

Two Bar Method

The two bar method is a quick and easy way of cross drilling and one jig will cope with a variety of sizes, it also provides a quick way to drill square or flat bar along the centre line.. Two pieces of square or rectangular steel bar will be needed, together with three identical lengths of flat stock. Again sizes are not of any great importance. Three evenly spaced holes are needed in the long pieces and these will all have to be tapped at a size to suit the work. Both pieces must of course be identical. The flat strips also need to be drilled, two require two holes and the other a third centrally between the two. It is essential that the outer holes in all three strips are identical in their placing.

Screw the parts together together leaving enough play for the parts to be folded together and opened out as required. Ordinary screws will work quite well but for long life it will be as well to make special screws from silver steel and harden them.

Two Bar Method

The photograph shows how the idea works, in this case on a piece of copper tubing. Cheesehead screws are used as pivots, they are sufficiently accurate for the purpose.

The round section to be cross drilled is laid along the inside of the tool and the centre hole used to drill through and as long as reasonable care has been taken when making the tool the hole will be exactly central across the work. The tools will work on a variety of diameters.

Bushes

If the previous two tools have a disadvantage, it is because the holes used for drilling soon wear out, something that can be cured by making drilling bushes, from silver steel. These require nothing more than a step turned on one end, to a length equal to the thickness of the crosspiece. At the same chuck setting drill a hole through of the required size, then part off. Reverse in the chuck and put in a good deep countersink.

The bush should now be hardened and the hole in the crosspiece reamed to size to accept the step on the bush. The latter should ideally be a force fit in the crosspiece but if not it can be held with a retaining compound. As with everything we do there is a snag, the tool is only suitable for drilling one diameter. Fortunately once a hole has been drilled through a piece of metal, if another drill is used to open the hole out it will exactly follow the line of the original hole. Of course if the hole required is smaller than the bush the system will not work. The best idea therefore is to drill the guide hole with a small drill and rely on opening if necessary.

Variation on The Theme

All the above suggestions work well enough for centrally cross drilling a

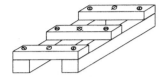

Two bar Type Cross Drilling Jig
In this case all three cross bars
are centrally drilled, allowing
spaced holes to also be drilled

The two bar type of jig is particularly useful for small work. It also has the advantage that it is equally effective on square and rectangular bar.

round bar. What if we do not need the hole to be central? Well there is one further idea that can be used both for central and offset drilling and is also very useful where rows of evenly spaced holes are needed. In addition it is the only type of cross drilling device that can be used on very thin rod, in fact it can even be used to cross drill wire if one wishes. Once again it is quite easy to make. Take two pieces of flat stock and join them together with screws. Put the piece in the lathe four jaw chuck and exactly on the join line drill a hole to the diameter of the bar to be worked on. Ideally this should go right through the length of the work and break out the other side. However if, for example a number of components are to be made with a hole at a specified distance from the end, then the hole through the work can be finished at a suitable point with a "D" bit

in order to get it nice and square and act as a stop.

Carefully mark and drill the position where holes will be needed in the work and drill the top of the jig to suit. Run the drill into the lower section as well. Finally remove the top section and deburr the edges of the main hole in which the work will be pushed and also the holes to be used as drilling guides. The holes for cross drilling should be very slightly countersunk to allow for any burr that might occur when the work is drilled. Once again this type of jig will benefit from the fitting of bushes if it is to be used for a lot of work.

With plenty of ideas on how to get the required accuracy, cross drilling should no longer appear to be the daunting operation it was once thought to be and can be tackled with complete confidence.

The type of jig illustrated above can give very high precision results and is particularly effective on very small diameter work.

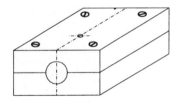

This type of cross drilling
jig has the advantage that
holes can be drilled to a
deliberate off-set. It is also
suitable fro cross drilling
very small work, even wire

A Filing Machine

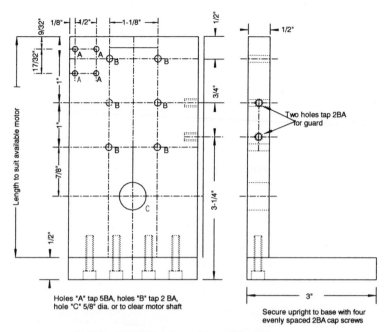

Holes "A" tap 5BA, holes "B" tap 2 BA,
hole "C" 5/8" dia. or to clear motor shaft

Two holes tap 2BA
for guard

Secure upright to base with four
evenly spaced 2BA cap screws

Length to suit available motor

PART 1 BODY, fabricate from mild steel

Most of us can use a file, although it is quite surprising how few people can use one really well. Old time engineers could file a piece of metal perfectly flat leaving virtually no file marks at all. The secret was in the method of holding the file, the fact that it was used on the forward stroke only and of course many years of experience. The standard tradesmans' test for many industries and at one time also for the armed forces, was to give the applicant a piece of round bar, of the same length as the diameter. The applicant had to file it to a perfect cube of a given size. The finished result to be perfectly square and all surfaces perfectly flat. In the case of an apprentice trying to pass his test, if it was not right he had to repeat the operation until it was. Nowadays of course the file is resorted to far less often, most work being carried out by high precision machinery. Only a fitter is likely to need to be highly skilled in filing.

Why then should we need a filing machine? The answer is that even with the increase in the quality of home machinery. It is still unlikely that most model engineers will always have the right equipment for a particular job. Odd shapes will need to be formed with a file and indeed it may even be quicker to do so. This particularly applies where small work is concerned. While logically it might seem that filing small areas is easier that filing large ones, this is not so. Most small work is done with needle files and it is all too easy to set these at a slight angle and ruin a piece of work.

The machine that is being described is made for use with needle files although it would be possible to increase the size to accept warding files if one so wishes. It has one disadvantage, but only a minor one, normal files will cut only on the up stroke. This means they are pushing the work away from the table when in use. It is possible to purchase special files that have the teeth formed in the opposite direction. However providing the work is held firmly against the table, cutting on the up stroke is no great problem.

This photograph clearly shows details of the sliding block assembly

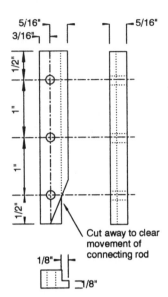

PART 2-GUIDES or RUNNERS two required- left and right handed. Make from mild steel. All holes 4 BA clear.

We are these days offered a very useful alternative. We can buy needle files that instead of having normal teeth are impregnated with either tungsten or diamond chips. These cut in either direction and it is worth considering their use.

The Motor

To build the machine an electric motor will be needed and this does not need to be very powerful. It is essential though that it should have a gear box fitted. The final rotation should be between a hundred and fifty and two hundred revolutions a minute. Such motors are not difficult to find, often

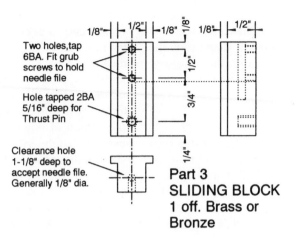

1/8" 1/2" 1/8" 1/8" 1/8" 1/2"

Two holes, tap
6BA. Fit grub
screws to hold
needle file

Hole tapped 2BA
5/16" deep for
Thrust Pin

1/2"

3/4"

Clearance hole
1-1/8" deep to
accept needle file.
Generally 1/8" dia.

1/4"

**Part 3
SLIDING BLOCK
1 off. Brass or
Bronze**

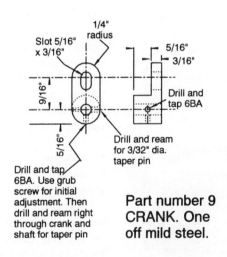

Slot 5/16"
x 3/16"

1/4"
radius

5/16"
3/16"

9/16"

Drill and
tap 6BA

5/16"

Drill and ream
for 3/32" dia.
taper pin

Drill and tap
6BA. Use grub
screw for initial
adjustment. Then
drill and ream right
through crank and
shaft for taper pin

**Part number 9
CRANK. One
off mild steel.**

they are sold as surplus material, being used in a variety of domestic and commercial appliances. The final size of the machine will depend on the size of the motor used, the height of the shaft and the measurements of the fixings.

The Body

The body is fabricated from two pieces of plate, these are both shown as being a half inch thick but in fact the original machine used three quarter thick plate for the upright, purely because a piece of such material hap-

The brackets and screws provide a mechanism for tilting the table to allow filing to be carried out at a precise angle if required. The photograph also shows how the guard is constructed and held in position

pened to be available. This should be marked out,drilled and tapped for the holes used to secure the slides and also the four used to hold the piece of angle at the back. A large hole will be needed to clear the motor shaft and this must be at the distance from the slides shown on the drawings. Once the position of this is established it is possible by reference to the motor to establish the length of the upright.

If need be, cut and machine the upright to the required length, then drill and tap for the screws that secure it to the base. Mark out,drill and counterbore the base, join the parts together with cap screws and check everything is square. If not make the necessary adjustments. The two parts can then be separated. The only other work needed on the base is tapped holes to secure the motor, the position of which cannot be given. Also some motors are not adequately covered and wires will be left exposed. In these cases it will be necessary to make a simple cover from a piece of folded mild steel and to screw this down, using a couple of small angle pieces.

The Slides

There are two ways of making the slides, they can be machined from a solid length of steel bar. or fabricated by screwing or riveting two pieces of bar together to form the necessary lip. If milling facilities are limited the latter idea is the easiest. Take a length of 3/4 ins. by 1/8 ins.. steel bar and mark off

USEFUL WORKSHOP TOOLS

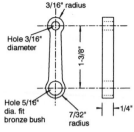

Hole 3/16" diameter

Hole 5/16" dia. fit bronze bush

3/16" radius

1-3/8"

7/32" radius

1/4"

2 BA

3/16" dia.

3/8" dia.

1/8"

1/4"

5/16"

THRUST PIN for sliding block 1 off from bronze. Part number 12

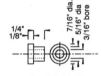

1/4"
1/8"

7/16" dia.
5/16" dia.
3/16" bore

CONNECTING ROD and BUSH Rod from mild steel. Bush bronze or brass Part number 11

it is a quite straightforward job to mill the groove. This should be dressed with a file if necessary to ensure that the sliding block will move smoothly up and down. If the groove is machined, almost certainly the slides will need to be made as two separate pieces. If the two part system is used it is a good idea to make a single length and cut it in half at a later stage. Finally, which ever method of construction has been used the bottom ends of the slides need to be tapered to clear the rotation of the connecting rod, this again can either be done on the milling machine or with a hack saw and file.

along the centre line at 3/4 ins. intervals for suitable holes. Either to be tapped, or clearance size for rivets. 5BA will be about right for screws and 1/8 ins.. for rivets. In the latter case the holes will need to be countersunk. Use some double sided adhesive tape to hold a length of 3/16 ins.. by 3/8 ins.. bar to it. having first thoroughly deburred it and cleaned both parts to ensure no grease remains. Transfer the holes through the second piece. Separate them, open the holes in the second piece to clearance size if screws are to be used and countersink on the underside. If screwing the parts together tap the top section. It is essential to ensure that any screw heads or rivets are flush or below the surface.

If the parts are to be machined then

Sliding Block

Once again we have two choices in the form of construction either to mill the grooves or fabricate. There is one major difference, if fabrication is chosen. It is not recommended to either screw or rivet the parts together. As

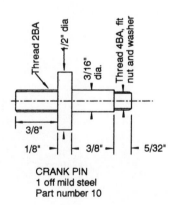

Thread 2BA

1/2" dia

3/16" dia.

Thread 4BA, fit nut and washer

3/8"

1/8"

3/8"

5/32"

CRANK PIN 1 off mild steel Part number 10

A small motor fitted with a gearbox, assembled to the machine. A cover is essential for such a motor and can be seen in the other photographs. The holes are duplicated on the other side to provide ventilation for the motor. The one which the wire for the motor passes through should be fitted with a grommet to protect the wire.

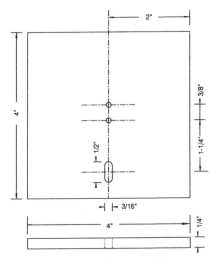

Part 6 TABLE 1 off Mild Steel

the component must, for the purpose of reducing wear, be made from brass or bronze the two sections should be soldered together. Soft soldering will be quite satisfactory and the best method of doing this is to 'tin' both components first, then heat them and allow them to settle together of their own accord.

Tinning

For anyone not familiar with the tinning process we will go through the procedure. Start by liberally covering the whole of each side to be joined with flux and then heat and apply solder. which should run across the whole component, although in all probability not very evenly. While the solder is still molten wipe it over using a clean brush, or piece of rag. The brushing must be light and take care

not to burn the material so that it fouls up the surface. The end result should be nice flat silver coloured surfaces. One of these can then be covered in flux, the two parts held together and the work heated until the line of solder at the join is seen to melt. Once cool they will be joined perfectly with no danger of them parting.

Trying to hold them together and allowing solder to run into the join is asking for trouble. Invariably some parts will not have solder adhering to them, giving the possibility of them parting when in use. It is also inclined to lead to an uneven join with one side of the work raised slightly higher than the other.

Drilling

There is very little work to be done on the sliding block once it has been shaped. two tapped holes will be needed to secure the file in position, which in itself needs a hole in the top of the block. Handles if indeed they can be called that on needle files, consist of a long round section. but this may vary according to the whim of the manufacturer. It also varies from metric to imperial measurements these days. Fortunately, while it is nice to have a good snug fit in the block a slight discrepancy will not matter and so it will be possible to use files with a slightly smaller diameter handle as well as the size for which the machine is intended. It is important that the hole is at an exact ninety degrees to the edge of the slide and so it should be drilled with the component mounted in the four jaw chuck of the lathe.

The Crank

The crank is made from a short length of mild steel bar 3/8 ins.. square. The circular section and the hole that will fit the motor shaft can be machined, using the four jaw chuck. The other end is slotted, the crank pin bolts to this and the slot can be made either by drilling two holes and then converting them with a file, alternatively it can be milled and it becomes just a case of rounding off the end, purely for the sake of appearance and this can quite easily be done with a file. It is secured to the motor shaft with a 3/32" taper pin after having been held in position for testing with a grub screw. This may sound unnecessarily complicated but a grub screw on its own is not sufficient to take the strain imposed by filing. Should the shaft be hardened then it

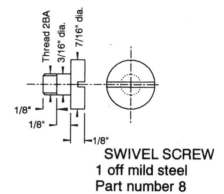

SWIVEL SCREW
1 off mild steel
Part number 8

will be as well to drill and tap the crank for two or if possible three grub screws which should hold it. Some shafts may be keyed, in which case the obvious answer is to make a keyway in the crank and key it to the shaft.

Crank Pin

This is a simple turning and threading exercise. The end with the plain section should be finished first and then the component turned round to machine and thread the other end.

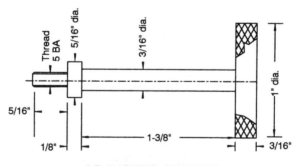

ADJUSTER SCREW
1 off mild steel
Part number 8

Standard nuts are all that is needed to secure it at each end.

Connecting Rod.

Providing a suitable accurate drilling machine is available the two holes can be drilled on that, they must be absolutely at ninety degrees to the shaft, so if you are not confident about the accuracy of the machine do them in the four jaw chuck. Apart from the two holes the only other work required is to shape the component. The bronze bush is an easy enough turning operation. It can be made a push fit in the connecting rod or it can be secured with a retaining compound. The thrust pin that holds the rod to the sliding block is made of bronze to avoid the necessity of bushing the other end.

Brackets

Two brackets are required both cut from one inch angle an eighth of an inch thick. The piece that bolts to the rear of the body has a hole and a curved slot in it. The latter can be made on a milling machine, using a rotary table, or it can be chain drilled and filed. When the bracket is fitted to the body it must lie absolutely flush with the top. This is in order to line it up with the other bracket which is screwed to the table. As well as acting as a support for the table the slotted one is used to adjust the tilt. This allows really accurate angular filing to be carried out.

The Table

Yet another piece of mild steel plate, the table has a short slot which allows

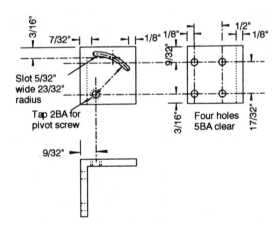

Part 4 FIXED BRACKET
Make from 1" x 1" x 1/8"
angle. Screw to body.

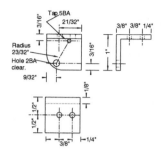

Part 5 BRACKET
I off from 1"X1"X1/8"
Mild Steel Angle screw
to table

the file to pass through, even when set at an angle. There are also two holes for securing it to the bracket. These apart the only other necessity is to ensure that the edges are square and that when assembled it lines up correctly. If this is not done properly, not only will the filing not be accurate, but there may also be a problem tilting the table to the required angle.

The Table Screws

Two screws are called for to hold the table in position, both are straight forward enough to make. It is possible to use a standard bolt instead of the swivel screw, shown in the drawings. It will not however be as accurate as the one shown which is designed to be a snug fit in the hole in the bracket. The adjuster screw needs to be of sufficient length for it to pass outside the table in order to easily tighten it when set at an angle. Although making it is a nice exercise in turning it would be

very easy to fabricate. This would involve securing the ring to the spindle with retaining compound and likewise the knurled handle. It is an idea worth pursuing if one doesn't want to machine large diameter material to a much smaller size for any reason.

The Guard

In this day and age safety is paramount and so a simple guard has been devised for the machine. It makes sense to use it as some needle files have a very sharp pointed ends and it would be possible to get a serious injury if one was to catch a person in the eye, or something similar. The guard screws to the side of the body and is mainly made from aluminium. The only reason for using this is the extreme difficulty in bending steel of this thickness with any degree of accuracy. As shown it is a nice sturdy job but if for any reason someone wishes to use steel then the thickness of the material could be reduced by a third or even a half, which will make it easier to bend.

The top of the guard consists of a steel block screwed to the upright and bored to accept a piece of tubing, which can be of any available material, or within reason any size that will allow the passage of a needle file. The hole in the block should be bored on the lathe to ensure it is square. The tube is held in place with a small knurled screw that allows the height to be adjusted as required.

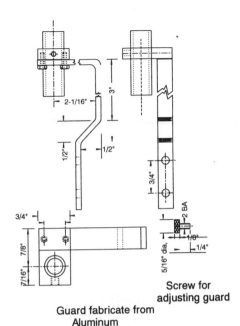

2-1/16"

3"

1/2" 1/2"

3/4"

2 BA

1/8"

5/16" dia, 1/4"

3/4"

7/8"

7/16"

Screw for
adjusting guard

Guard fabricate from
Aluminum

Assembly

Many readers will devise their own method of assembly. For those who are not sure how to go about it, the drawings give what is considered to be the best method.

Start with the body, bolting the two sections together. At this stage it might be prudent to check the fitting of the motor and make sure the shaft lines up centrally with the hole. If satisfied, assemble the slides to the body, before doing so ensure that the bearing surfaces of the slides are nice and smooth. All milling marks must be removed as otherwise they will wear the sliding block out in no time at all. Give them a final rub with a very fine emery paper to just make sure that

they will really be smooth. Put a shake proof washer on each bolt before tightening it up. The slides are subject to a great deal of vibration and will easily work loose.

Slip in the sliding block, after once again ensuring the the bearing surfaces really are smooth, If there are any tight spots ease them out with a file, or emery cloth. Make sure that needle files will fit properly without too much shake when the screws are tightened. Bolt on the bracket and check with a square that it lies parallel to the top of the body upright. Check also that the face is at ninety degrees. A lot of angle iron, even the bright type will be found to be far from that. If there is any problem put the angle in the four jaw chuck and machine the side that will be bolted to the body to the correct angle. Make sure the face is nice and smooth so that it will rotate easily and of course the same will apply when we come to the second piece of angle.

The second stage of assembly involves fitting the crank, etc. to the motor and sliding block so obviously we now need the motor in position and the crank secured to it. Assemble the connecting rod to the crank and sliding block and rotate the motor to ensure everything runs free.

Screw the second bracket to the underside of the table, after making sure it is square and polished as in the first case. It is then just a case of joining the table to the body using

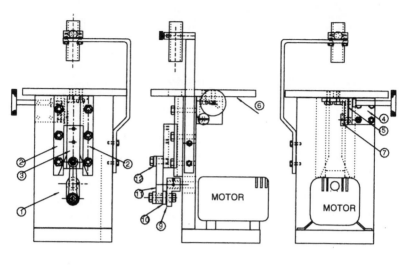

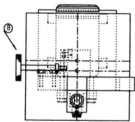

General arrangement of Filing Machine, including guard.

the two screws.

Depending on the type of motor it may be necessary to make a cover. certainly if it is similar to the one shown in the photograph it would be highly dangerous to leave it exposed. It is not at all difficult to make a cover as it is simply a piece of sheet metal folded round the motor to give a reasonable clearance and a piece soldered on the end to cover that. Although not fitted when the photographs were taken rubber grommets should be put in any holes to prevent chafing of the cable.

The machine will accept any shape of needle file and is useful for making gentle radii, either inside or outside. It is of particular use to horologists when crossing out clock wheels, etc. Model ship builders and people interested in making small model locomotives, etc. will also find that it can help to get accuracy to small parts Although such things as clocks and small models immediately spring to mind it is also useful for larger items such as locomotives and traction engines in the construction of fittings to complete the model.

Setting Up Aids

A spring loaded setting up tool as described below. Note short length of probe, to prevent excessive wear. The point should be hardened and tempered, again to prevent wear.

When work is put in the four jaw chuck of the lathe it becomes necessary to find the exact position of the centre of the piece we wish to machine. usually this will be done on the bench before putting the work in the chuck and is indicated by a centre punch mark. We are then left with the problem of how to ensure that the mark is truly in the centre.

Setting Up

Let us retrace our steps a little and try and get it nearly right in the first place. It is surprising just how far out off line it is possible to be when a piece of work is chucked and lined up by eye. If we take a piece of mild steel, say about six inches or a hundred and fifty millimetres in length and of a diameter of about a quarter of an inch or six mil-

limetres. We put a point on one end at an angle of roughly sixty degrees and we already have something that will help. Put that in the tailstock chuck and when the work is chucked it will be possible to see where the centre mark is in relation to the point.

This position will not be correct by any means but it will be a lot nearer than working by eye. To true the work up, the lathe will need to be rotated by hand and we need something a little more accurate than our piece of pointed steel. In fact we need something that will rotate with the work and then the amount of eccentricity can be measured. The piece of steel cannot do this because it is rigidly held in the tailstock chuck. If we were to put a small centre in the plain end and support that end with a tailstock centre, it

**Setting Up Tool (Type One)
General Arrangement**

Pointer 1 off- silver steel
Harden and temper light blue

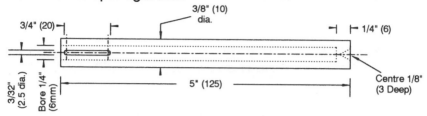

Body for Setting Up Tool, (1st type)

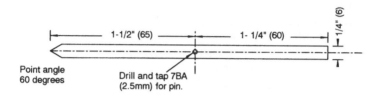

Point angle
60 degrees

Drill and tap 7BA
(2.5mm) for pin.

would become possible to see what movement there was at the chuck end. So far so good, except that being rigid, if the point moves too far off centre the piece of rod will fall out. Even so the idea does work and in an emergency it is possible to replace the metal rod with another lathe centre and suspend that between the work and the tailstock centre.

Spring Loading

To stop it falling out, we can use a device that is spring loaded. These are not at all difficult to make and two different versions are shown in the drawings, although only one appears in the photographs. The first type consists of a piece of round stock, which we will call the body, with a centre in one end, and drilled out to most of its length. A

short slot is milled in the open end. The pointer or probe, whatever one likes to call it needs to be a good sliding fit in the body, but there must be no shake. A pin that is a nice running fit in the slot that has been milled, is screwed into the probe after it has been put in the body. Before putting it in insert a length of spring and we

Using a clock gauge with the setting up tool, in order to achieve absolute accuracy.

One of the spring-loaded tools being used in conjunction with a scribing block to set up work in the lathe

ment. An end cap is made which will fit over the pointer, once again as a nice sliding fit and screw into the body. It is shown in the drawings as knurled but there is no reason why a piece of hexagon should not be used, allowing it to be tightened up with a spanner. Once again a spring is inserted in between body end and probe before assembly and we have a spring loaded setting up device.

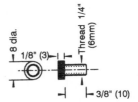

End cap. As an alternative to knurling, use hexagon.

have our spring loaded setting up device. The point or probe should not be allowed to extend too far from the end of the body or excessive wear will be created over a period of time.

Type Two

The second version is a little more complicated to make, but it is still easy. We again need a tube with a centre in the end but this time instead of a slot the open end is tapped. The pointer is set into a length of round stock that is a nice sliding fit in the tube, again without any sideways move-

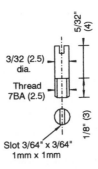

Pin 1 Off Mild Steel

Fit 18 gauge spring
7/32" (5) O/D 1-1/2"
(40) long

Setting Up Aid Type 2
General Arrangement

3/8" (10)
Thread this end
1/4" (6mm) by
3/8" (10) deep

2 -5/8" (65)

3/8" (10)
O/side dia. 5/16"(8mm)
bore 7/32" (5) small
centre in end

Setting Up Tool (2nd type)
Body from Mild Steel

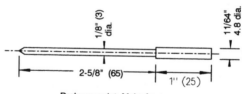

1/8" (3) dia.

11/64" 4.8 dia.

2-5/8" (65)

1" (25)

Probe or point. Make from
silver steel, harden and temper

The second version has some advantages over the first. For a start it is possible to have a much thinner probe as the support is supplied with the top cap and the internal part of the probe itself. The type therefore lends itself more readily to use on a the very small lathes. In both instances it will pay to keep a little drop of oil or grease in the tube so that the probe is a good sliding fit.

To use the tools it is best to start checking with a scribing block and then subsequently when adjustment from the scriber has reached its limit, to use a clock gauge to get perfect accuracy.

A Hand Turning Rest

The hand turning rest seen from the rear. It consists of only two basic parts, both of which are fabricated.

Wood turners invariably use hand tools for their work and to do so they use a hand tool rest. We only have to look at the output of many of them to admire their skill and dexterity. Of course they are generally using much softer materials than the model engineer and also the generating of straight lines is not so important.

There are times when using their methods for our purposes can pay dividends, particularly where awkward shapes are concerned. If the right equipment is available machining a curve is not all that difficult, problems arise when there is an immediate need to reverse the curve and in particular where a gentle transition into and out

For polishing round bar. Stick
polishing material, emery, etc...
to strip of flat wood and use
as shown in the drawing.

of a curved surface are needed.

The usual way to deal with that situation is to make a template of the line of the curve, machine as near to it as possible and then finish with a file. Offering the template to the work at frequent intervals, as a means of checking accuracy. The template does not have to be substantial for a one off effort. It can even be cut from a piece of card. The machining will also be straightforward enough. It is when it comes to finishing with a file that the fun starts. No matter how careful the operator is, or what grade of file is used it will almost certainly leave nasty marks in the work. The next step is to use an abrasive cloth or paper to try and get a decent finish.

Careful use of a hand turning tool can give both accuracy and finish with a little effort. It will more often than not still be wise to carry out normal machining operations in the first place in order to save hard work. The template is also just as essential as an aid to accuracy, in every other respect hand turning is far superior to trying to fins work with a file.

The tools needed for metal work are very similar to those used by the wood worker. They are long and securely embedded in a handle. The cutting edge is ground to roughly the same angles as those of a normal turning tool, but the shape will usually be rounded. The tools must be used at centre height and at an angle of about thirty degrees. It will depend on the depth of cut as to how much force will be needed but in general the rule must be to use very light cuts. If the tool is going to snag, it will be a good bet that it will do so when the operator is relaxing and off guard. A time when it will be all too easy for an accident to happen.

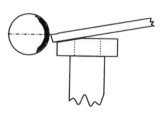

When removing metal, the rest should be arranged so that it is as close to the work as possible. Leaving a gap can result in the tool jamming under the work. Ensure that the cutting edge of the tool is at the lathe centre height, for best results.

A view of the rest from the other side, showing the sloping edge.

Making The Rest.

The rest consists of two basic parts, each of which will also consist of two parts, so making it is only going to be a couple of hours work. It is an ideal project for a beginner, as well as being a chance to use up odd pieces of bar and rod.

The Base

The sizes shown on the drawings are suitable for a small lathe, people with larger machines should increase sizes proportionally. Machine a step in a piece of round bar and bore right through it. Make sure it is a nice substantial thickness as the screw that will lock the table in position will need to have plenty of metal to grip in to. When the lathe work is finished cross drill and tap it for the locking screw.

Take a piece of flat bar and using the four jaw chuck, bore a hole to take the step turned in the piece of bar. It must be a good fit. Finally drill two holes for the bolts hat will hold it to the cross slide.

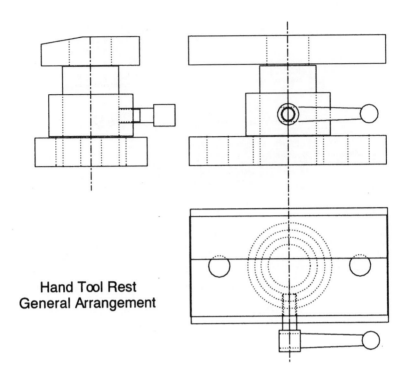

**Hand Tool Rest
General Arrangement**

The Table

We need a piece of flat bar and a suitable hole should be bored in it using the lathe. It is tempting to use a drilling machine for this sort of job but they do not always drill all that accurately. It will be a far better job if placed in the four jaw chuck, with the jaws reversed, using the steps as locating points. The only other work required on this piece is to machine an angle along one edge. Ideally this should be at about ten degrees, but a degree or two out will not make the slightest bit of difference. This chamfer can be made with the work held crosswise at an angle in the milling vice. or it can be held at an angle in the four jaw chuck of the lathe and finished that way.

A pillar goes in the hole A good guide of the length required for your particular lathe is the centre height, from the cross slide, minus the thickness of the tool table and a quarter of an inch or six millimetres. In other words if the height of the centre above

the cross slide is two inches and a piece of half inch plate is being used for the table, The pillar will need to be one and a half inches or twelve millimetres, minus a quarter inch or six millimetres. A step is turned to a good fit in the hole in the table. Care must be taken to get the length of the step exactly right as we do not want a recess left in the table top. If you are not too sure about getting things that accurate make it so it will protrude above the table and after assembly either mill or turn it flush to the table

Assembly

Both parts need to be assembled and ideally they should be brazed together. If the fit is right, they can be secured with a retaining compound and to be successful there should be a gap of about two thousandths of an

inch or about 0.02mm. If the parts are too tight the adhesive will not have room to get around the parts and do its job. If they are too loose then it will be too thin to adhere to both surfaces.

Locking Bolt

A locking screw is needed to enable the table height to be adjusted. An ordinary bolt can be used although over a period this will mark the pillar to such an extent that it will be almost unuseable. For that reason a locking bolt was made from brass, once again it was fabricated and it is not difficult to do. A length of brass was machined to size and threaded to fit the base. It was then cross drilled.

Another length of brass was tuned down so that one end was a nice fit in the cross drilled hole referred to

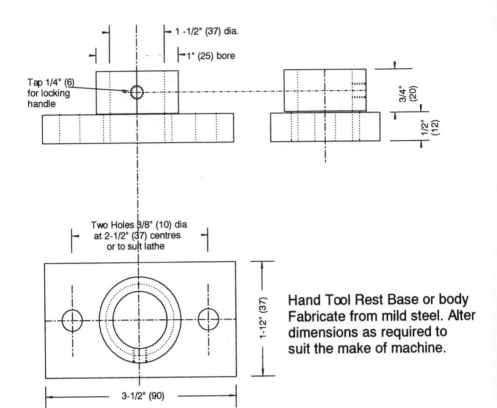

1-1/2" (37) dia.

1" (25) bore

Tap 1/4" (6) for locking handle

3/4" (20)

1/2" (12)

Two Holes 3/8" (10) dia at 2-1/2" (37) centres or to suit lathe

1-12" (37)

3-1/2" (90)

Hand Tool Rest Base or body Fabricate from mild steel. Alter dimensions as required to suit the make of machine.

above., The other end was tapered by about two degrees and a piece left at the end to be machined as a sphere. A hand tool was used to make the sphere. This brings us to a chicken and egg situation where we need a hand turning rest to make a part for a hand turning rest. Actually it is not like that at all as we can use the one we have just made and secure it with an ordinary bolt. To prevent marking the pillar put in a couple of thicknesses of paper or a piece of brass

shim. It will last long enough to do the job and that is all we need.

Ball Turning Tool

The tool used to make the sphere is a very simple one made from a length of silver steel. Take piece about a half inch or 12mm diameter and drill a hole three eigths of an inch or 10mm diameter and the same depth. You now have a simple ball turning tool or at least will once it is hardened and tempered to a dark straw colour. Machine

USEFUL WORKSHOP TOOLS

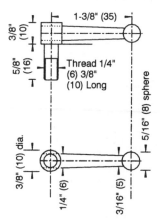

Locking Screw. One off- Brass. Alternatively use Aluminum. Do not under any circumstances use steel as it will mark the pillar and make future height adjustments difficult.

the other end to a small enough diameter to fit a standard file handle and secure one on it with an epoxy adhesive. To use it start by removing the square corners and then slowly rotate the tool as it presses against the metal. The idea quickly becomes obvious and you will be amazed at how simple it is to machine a sphere in this way.

It goes without saying that all the tools that are used will need to be considerably longer than the normal turning tool, about seven to eight inches or a hundred and sixty millimetres or so is ideal. Handles must be securely in place and for safety should be retained with an adhesive suitable for the job. Long lengths of high speed steel can be bought or alternatively hardened and tempered tools of silver steel can be used. Probably though the best idea is to use mild steel with a flat machined on the end and carbide tip brazed on. The flat must be exactly that. Perfectly flat. Do not try and file it, if it is not absolutely flat before brazing takes place the tip will almost certainly break when it is under pressure.

Using The Rest

How to use the rest has already been mentioned but there are a few points worth remembering. Firstly ensure the the table is as close to the work as possible and that the cutting edge of the tool will be at centre height when used. There is a danger of the tool sliding underneath if the table is too far from the work. One job that the rest copes with particularly well is polishing. For this we do need the table a little further away than usual. Use a piece of fine abrasive paper or cloth stuck to a strip of wood fit it below the work as shown in the drawing. Under no circumstances should metal be used as a base for the abrasive.

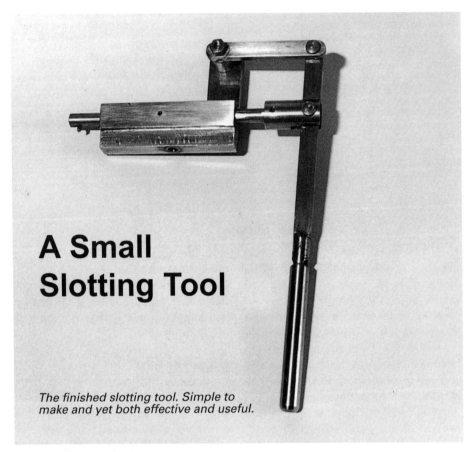

A Small
Slotting Tool

The finished slotting tool. Simple to make and yet both effective and useful.

Slotting tools are designed to do just what the name suggests, cut slots. Generally speaking in the model-engineering world we do not need to cut very long or deep slots, they are usually required for internal keyways or perhaps occasionally for making a spline. Outside keyways and splines can more often than not be made with a milling cutter. Normally a key-way tool is a pretty hefty affair and if used on the lathe a weighty casting is bolted to the bed as the basis for the construction. In industry a special machine would normally be used. For the type of slots we require it is certainly not necessary to go to these lengths and this design works from the tool post. An added advantage being that there is no reason to remove the tool post in order to use it. One thing is important though, and that is the fact that the cross slide must be firmly locked in position to use the tool. If not it will be inclined to

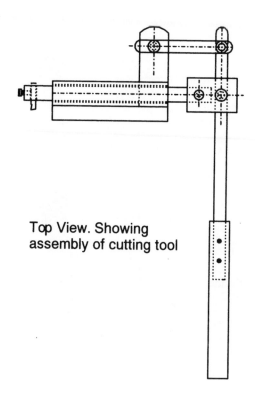

Top View. Showing
assembly of cutting tool

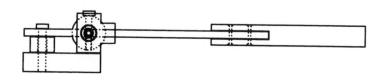

**General view of completed slotting tool
from the mandrel end.**

move away from the work as pressure is applied. That apart and providing there is no attempt to make cuts that are too deep for the tool to cut, it works very well indeed. No castings are needed and most of the materials will be found in the average workshop.

This slotting tool is designed to machine slots 0f 1/8 or 5/32ins (3 or 4mm) width and the size of the ram is such that this should not be exceeded.

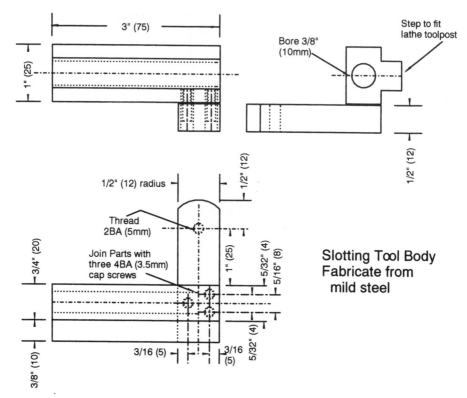

3" (75)

1" (25)

Bore 3/8"
(10mm)

Step to fit
lathe toolpost

1/2" (12)

1/2" (12) radius

1/2" (12)

Thread
2BA (5mm)

3/4" (20)

Join Parts with
three 4BA (3.5mm)
cap screws

1" (25)

5/32" (4)

5/16" (8)

**Slotting Tool Body
Fabricate from
mild steel**

3/8" (10)

3/16 (5)

3/16
(5)

5/32" (4)

It does lend itself to resizing and as long as proportions are reasonably near to being the same considerably larger versions can be made. Even so it is not advisable to go too large as the strain created on the top slide and lead screw could be too great and damage to the lathe could occur.

The Body

The body is made from a piece of rectangular bar, and although dimensions are given, within reason almost any piece of similar bar can be used. It needs to be drilled for the ram and the hole must be on or slightly below the lathe centre height. Although shown plain it would be an advantage if the hole was made large enough to fit a bronze bearing as it would save a lot of wear and tear.

The drawings also show a section milled out in order that the body will fit a four-way tool post. Like most things this will depend on the lathe for which the tool is being made. Some will not have this type of tool holder and perhaps the tool holding arrangements will be a simple screw down clamp. If so the step should be ignored and the bar left plain. For lathes that have a simple clamp down arrangement of tool holding, a hefty piece of bar will be required. This is certainly not a disadvantage as the heavier and more solid the tool the better.

Fitted to the body is another length of bar which is screwed in position. It is best to use hexagon cap head screws and counterbore so they fit snugly in the recess. This will provide a much firmer fitting than an ordinary bolt, as the recess pushing against the cap head also acts to restrain any movement, so the better the cap fits the more secure the job will be. It must be born in mind that there is a considerable strain on this bar when the tool is in use.

Spacer and Pivot Pin

The bar referred to above has a tapped hole in it and this accepts the pin that will act as a pivot for the operating bar. As there is a discrepancy in height between these two a spacer will also be needed. Neither of these components should need any manufacturing description as they are very straightforward. The spacer can be made of mild steel but the pin must be made from bronze. Three pins will be required in all and they all differ slightly.

Pivot Bar

This is a plain piece of mild steel bar with two holes drilled in it. They are clearance holes for the pivot pins and should there-

This photograph shows the assembly of the slotting tool. A pin with a nut has been used rather than pin number one shown on the drawing. There is an oil hole in the body to allow the ram to be oiled. The large hole in the body has no significance, the tool was made from scrap steel which happened to have the hole in it.

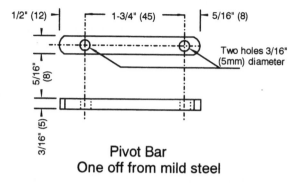

Pivot Bar
One off from mild steel

Dimensions shown: 1/2" (12), 1-3/4" (45), 5/16" (8), Two holes 3/16" (5mm) diameter, 5/16" (8), 3/16" (5)

fore be a good fit, even possibly a little on the tight side as a start. When the tool is in use, this and the operating lever take a lot of strain and so do not be tempted to make the pivot bar of flimsy material. By all means adapt to whatever material is to hand, but this is one instance where it will not be advisable to use a thinner material. There is no reason of course why thicker steel should not be used and suitable adjustments made to the length of the pivot pins.

Operating Bar

The bar provides the leverage for cutting the slot and again takes a good bit of strain. The tapped hole should be made with a taper tap and not passed completely through the work, this will then allow the pivot thread to bind in tight and prevent it from coming undone in use. If we were to lengthen the bar greater leverage would be applied, making the physical work of slot cutting easier. A slight increase can be gained by fitting a handle which is described later. Extending it must not be overdone as it will create far too

much pressure on other componenets and ultimately defeat its own purpose

The Ram

The part that will eventually provide the thrust, the ram is made from a length of mild or silver steel. In one end is a square hole to accept the tool bit and at right angles to that a tapped one for a screw to hold the tool in position. The square hole will almost certainly have to be filed to shape and this is not as easy as it sounds. Start by cross drilling the bar to the diameter of the proposed square. Filing will need to be carefully done and it will probably be as well to work from both ends. The little filing machine could do a very good job here as it will ensure that the file remains in a straight line when being used.

As a support, whether filing by hand or using the machine it will be a good idea to drill centrally through a piece of flat bar and cross drill for a screw. Slide the bar through leaving as little protruding as possible and slip a short length of round bar in the hole that has been drilled ready for the filing process.

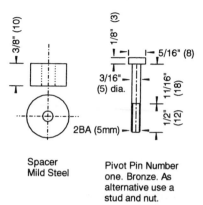

Spacer
Mild Steel

Pivot Pin Number
one. Bronze. As
alternative use a
stud and nut.

Lay the work on the bench in such a position that the round bar is vertical. Use a square to get it at a perfect ninety degrees. If necessary hold flat stock against the protruding piece and then the square against that as an extra guide.

Use the flat stock to hold the bar while filing operations are carried out. There is yet another dodge than can be used to assist in getting a nice square hole, assuming you do not have a filing machine. Put a square needle file in the drilling machine chuck and using the flat block as support, pass the file through the hole, and run it up and down using the drilling machine. But don't switch on of course. This is not good engineering practice as the file is supposed to work only in one direction and bringing it back in contact with the metal will cause wear. It is not easy using the drilling machine to work in one direction only but while it will not do the file a great deal of good it will assist in making a nice square hole.

There is one more little dodge that can be used to help get a nice square hole. Mark the size of square that is required and then draw diagonals to the four corners. Drill small holes on the diagonals and then drill in the centre of the square hole of the scme diameter as the square will be. It will break into the four hole, leaving little metal to be removed. Mind you in this size it is a rather fiddly way of going about things. Drawings are shown for anyone that wants to use the idea and the sizes shown are suitable for a 5/32 ins. or 4mm square.

The other end of the ram is fitted with a block to support the operating lever. It is shown as round, but can just as easily be made from flat or square stock. It can be riveted to the ram or better still brazed to it, either way it must be parallel with it. The original was fitted by means of a single grub screw, but this was later changed to a brazed joint. Before doing this it needs to be slotted, drilled and tapped. The top part is drilled clearance size with the lower half tapped for the pivot pin.

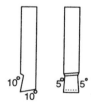

Tool bit, showing
shape required,
grind from high
speed steel. Size
to suit slot.

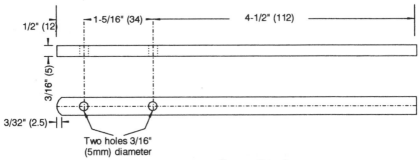

1/2" (12) 1-5/16" (34) 4-1/2" (112)

3/16" (5)

3/32" (2.5)

Two holes 3/16"
(5mm) diameter

Operating bar
One off from mild steel

Pins

One of the pins has already been referred to, two more are required. One joins the operating bar to the pivot bar and the other the operating bar to the ram. Both are straightforward turning operations and both should be made of bronze to give a good bearing surface. The tops can be slotted if one wishes to allow ease of assembly. The threads should be full and those that they mate with a little on the tight side. A great deal of pressure is created on them and if the threads are not a good fit the pins will almost certainly come loose.

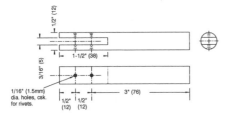

1/2" (12)

3/16" (5)

1-1/2" (38)

1/16" (1.5mm)
dia. holes, csk.
for rivets.

1/2" 1/2"
(12) (12)

3" (76)

Handle One off, mild steel.

A Handle

Left as it is the slotting tool is ready for use but after a while the flat section operating bar tends to become very uncomfortable. To avoid this a small mild steel handle was fitted. It consists only of a piece of round bar with a slot and a couple of holes which are countersunk each side. These are used for rivets with which it is secured to the operating bar. The rivets need to be well smoothed off or they too are likely to cause pain and possibly injury to ones hands.

Assembly

There really is little in the way of assembly to comment on. The two drawings show quite clearly what is required, which is just to fit the pieces together and tighten the screws.

Cutting Tool

High speed, or better still tungsten carbide is needed for the tool. It should be ground to a square shape for normal key cutting but there may be occasions

58

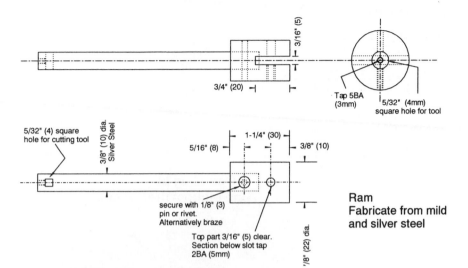

3/16" (5)

3/4" (20)

Tap 5BA
(3mm)

5/32" (4mm)
square hole for tool

5/32" (4) square
hole for cutting tool

3/8" (10) dia.
Silver Steel

5/16" (8)

1-1/4" (30)

3/8" (10)

secure with 1/8" (3)
pin or rivet.
Alternatively braze

Top part 3/16" (5) clear.
Section below slot tap
2BA (5mm)

1/8" (22) dia.

Ram
Fabricate from mild
and silver steel

when a special shape is called for. If Tungsten Carbide is used, it will of course have to be ground to shape with a green grit wheel. If a Tungsten tool is used then there is no need to use cutting fluid otherwise its use will be a definite advantage.

Usage

Using the tool is pretty straightforward. Because it is of a lightweight construction care must be taken not to attempt taking cuts that are too deep. In practice it probably will just not move along the work anyway if such an attempt is made. Ensure that the tool post and cross slide are tightened well up to stop it moving out of line during operations. If it is possible to drill a hole first so that only the edges of the slot need to be taken out. Remember at all times that a lot of strain is involved in this sort of operation, so take it easy.

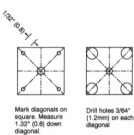

1/32" (0.8)

Mark diagonals on square. Measure 1.32" (0.8) down diagonal.

Drill holes 3/64" (1.2mm) on each diagonal

Drill 5/32" (4mm) to break into previously drilled holes. File out rest of metal

Possible method to be used
for making square hole for tool.

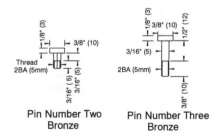

1/8" (3)

3/8" (10)

Thread
2BA (5mm)

3/16" (5)
3/16" (5)

Pin Number Two
Bronze

1/8" (3)

3/8" (10)

1/2" (12)

3/16" (5)

2BA (5mm)

3/8" (10)

Pin Number Three
Bronze

External Chuck Stop

Photograph demonstrating the general construction of the external chuck stop. The legs on this example were first pinned in position and then brazed.

Time and time again we find there is a necessity to repeat operations as more than one example of a particular item is required. There are all sorts of jigs that can be made to assist in this but none will be of any use unless the work can be placed in the machine in exactly the same position every time and this can only be achieved by the use of guides and stops.

This chapter is about making a stop to allow work to protrude a certain distance from the chuck jaws, elsewhere there is a description of another type of stop that allows work to be pushed into the chuck to the same depth in each operation. Of course there are other ways of getting work to protrude at a certain distance, we can for instance use a ruler and simply measure how far it sticks out, or perhaps machine a piece of metal to a specific length and use that as a guide. Both ways leave a lot to be desired as far as accuracy is concerned. The simple tool described here takes all the guesswork out of the job and makes repetition of setting very easy. The tool itself is about as simple as it could possibly be consisting only of six easily made parts.

The Body

The body, if we may call it that, is made from a piece of round bar about 6mm or 1/4 inch in thickness and although a diameter is shown on the drawings this may be varied at will to suit a particular type of lathe. The size shown was that used for a three-inch diameter chuck, larger sizes will need a larger diameter body and the small compact lathes a smaller diameter. Whilst the thickness will suit larger diameters, if smaller ones are to be used it may be as well to reduce the thickness of the plate by about a quarter.

Four holes are needed, three near the outside diameter for the legs and one in the centre for the adjusting screw. The central one should obviously be drilled and tapped while in the lathe, the others need to be marked off and drilled elsewhere. The three holes are not all that critical when it comes to spacing and to prevent having to set up a dividing device

the chuck jaws can be used for the purpose.

Hole Spacing

Put a piece of hardwood or metal on the lathe bed so that one chuck jaw when resting on it will be level. or near enough so. Rotate the chuck so the second jaw rests on the block and ditto for the third. Mark the position of the holes using some sort of guide. There are two ways of ensuring accuracy. The easiest is to drill a piece of square or rectangular bar using the four jaw chuck and make a centre punch from silver steel that will slide through it. Harden the punch and temper it to a dark straw colour. It is a simple job to mount the bar stock in the tool post, push in the centre punch and give it a sharp tap with a hammer.

The second device consists again of a piece of bar stock with a hole drilled in it. In both these instances the way to ensure the hole is at centre height is to put the drill in the lathe chuck and wind the tool post towards it, drilling the hole with the bar stock held firmly in the tool post. Having achieved a nice central hole, drill a piece of round bar to accept a small centre drill and at the other end make a handle of some sort. This can either be a proper handle or the bar can be cross-drilled and a piece of metal pushed through. The latter idea does not look so good but will do the job.

The centre drill is locked into the round stock or mandrel as it has now

Another view of the completed chuck stop. Should the need arise to set a stop for work protruding further from the chuck, it is simple enough to make extensions for the legs.

become, either by securing it with a retaining compound or cross drilling and tapping a hole and holding it with a screw. The device is used by rotating the handle with the centre drill pushed against the work and this makes a nice clean mark ready for drilling.

The Legs

Once again these are straightforward enough. The drawings show them screwed into the body and that is really quite sufficient. For those who like a belt and braces job there is no reason why they should not be silver soldered in position. Indeed there is

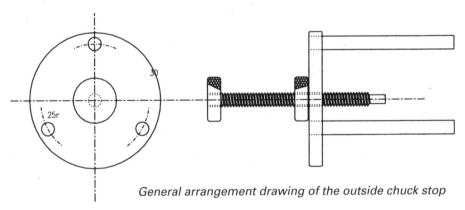

General arrangement drawing of the outside chuck stop

USEFUL WORKSHOP TOOLS

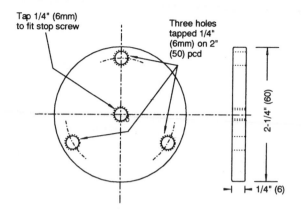

Tap 1/4" (6mm) to fit stop screw

Three holes tapped 1/4" (6mm) on 2" (50) pcd

2-1/4" (60)

1/4" (6)

External Chuck Stop Body . One Off from mild steel.

even a case for both screwing and silver soldering, the threads ensuring that the legs are at ninety degrees to the body and the silver soldering giving security. One thing that is absolutely certain is that all three must protrude to exactly the same length, otherwise accuracy will be impaired.

Stop Screw

Those who do not care for threading long pieces of steel could consider using a piece of studding for this and brazing the knurled top in position. Otherwise apart from a short length at the end where the thread is machined off the part is very straightforward to make. The top is shown as being knurled and for most work this will be a perfectly satisfactory arrangement. If anyone wishes to get a higher

degree of precision from the stop then instead of knurling the collar the side face can be marked in graduations, ten for a metric thread and twenty-five for the Imperial version. If these divisions are set against a mark on the body it will be possible to

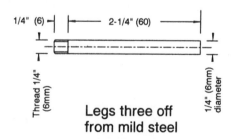

1/4" (6) 2-1/4" (60)

Thread 1/4" (6mm)

1/4" (6mm) diameter

Legs three off from mild steel

The legs can be made longer to cope with extra long work if one wants to. It will also mean extending the stop screw to cater for the extra length, A good alternative is to make three extensions into which the legs can fit.

The nut and stop screw should be knurled, to give a good grip. Diamond or straight knurling can be used.

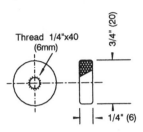

Locking Collar

adjust the stop to either a tenth of a millimetre or a thousandth of an inch.

Locking Collar
The only other remaining part is the locking collar and again this is quite straightforward and easy to make. Simply drill and tap a short length of bar, knurl it and then part off and the job is finished.

Usage
To use the stop it is as well to have a length of rod that will pass through the mandrel and chuck jaws with which to push the work up to it. Trying to put the work in the chuck and then slide it back towards the headstock, using the stop, almost invariably results in the work going too far in and we end up with the situation of pulling it out and pushing it in several times until it is right. Using a length of thin bar allows the work to be set forward in the chuck jaws slightly further than necessary. The stop is then set in position and in doing so there will usually be a sort of bounce effect that will push the work back a lttle further than required. The rod can then be used to push it back again and hard up to the stop. It sounds complicated but it isn't really and it does ensure accuracy. As it can be difficult at times to slide such a rod through the mandrel and into the chuck jaws, because it catches on the back of them, it is worth while putting on a slight taper that will allow it to slide through wihtout catching. Do not bring it right to a point as that could cause damage, just round the end slightly and it will work fine.

By using a thread such as 1/4" x40 or 6 x1 mm the amount of alteration to the position of the stop screw can be calculated.

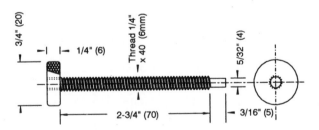

Stop Screw- Mild Steel

An Internal Chuck Stop

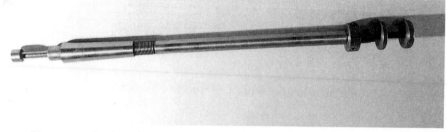

Photograph showing make up of the inside chuck stop.

We have already discussed in the previous chapter the need for some form of help in re-setting work to the same position and in that instance it was aimed at getting the work to protrude a predetermined distance from the chuck jaws. In this chapter the subject of setting work in the chuck to a set distance is dealt with.

For example a component may have been machined to a certain diameter which then needs a specially shaped recess set into it. The recess would be made with a tool known as a form tool. A rather technical sounding name for a simple cutting tool ground specially to shape. It is extremely difficult to measure each individual part in order to locate the second tool at exactly the same position on the work. Even with a changeable tool post this is far from easy. If we could set the work to a known distance in the chuck then the second tool can be set in position at the right place and each part will be exactly the same.

It is quite feasible to make a simple Morse Taper and set a bolt in it with the head at a predetermined distance and use that and it will work quite well. If the idea has any disadvantages it is in the fact the the taper is likely to move a tiny distance further in as the stop is used. It will not be a very great distance but nevertheless it will makea difference if we are working to very fine limits.

This problem can be solved by using a draw bar to pull the taper tight into the mandrel and the original design for this type of stop which was published in a a very early edition of the magazine, "Model Engineers' Workshop" was designed in exactly that way. After an extended period of use it became obvious that adjusting the depth from inside the chuck jaws was not a very clever idea. It meant working by trial and error. Taking the work out, adjusting the stop, putting the work back in and checking the distance it protruded. If it was not quite right out came the work again and another adjustment was made and so it went on and some-

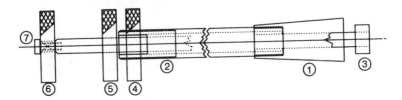

General Arrangement of inside chuck stop

times on and on.

An amendment has been made to the original published design that allows the stop to be adjusted from the rear of the machine using a simple hand wheel, which is a far more civilised arrangement. It is also far quicker to assemble than the original design. Measurements supplied are generally right for lathes of about three to three and a half inch centre height. People with larger or smaller lathes will need to make the necessary adjustments. This is not too difficult to do as the whole project is built round a morse taper. Number two has been used to set the standard and measurements can be scaled proportionally if a machine has another size of taper.

Morse Taper

The stop is built around a Morse Taper, part number one on the drawings. The simple form of construction is fully described in the chapter on a tailstock supported knurling tool, so it is not proposed to go through that procedure again. In this instance it is an advantage to shorten the taper at the narrow end as it has to be threaded. It

also needs to be bored right through, for the actual stop.

Support Tube Part 2

If a tube of suitable size is available, for part two, then go ahead and use it. If not it is going to be made from solid bar. The diameter must be a fraction under that of the mandrel bore. Unless you are working on a watchmakers' lathe the component will have to be drilled from each end, hoping that the drill will go deep enough to break into the hole in the other side. An extra long series would almost certainly work for most lathes. If an ordinary long series or perhaps an extra long series drill does not do the job try making an extension. Usually to do this we drill a piece of bar and fix the drill in that to use it. In this case as space is at at something of a premium it will be necessary to work the other way round. The shank of a drill will need drilling to accept a rod.

Assuming that say a 5/16 ins. or 8mm drill is to be used. Put it in the lathe chuck and drill a quarter inch diameter for about one and a quarter inches. The shank end should be quite

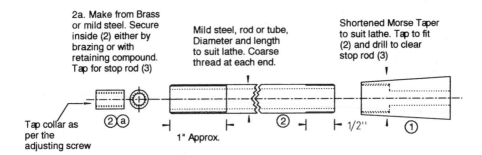

2a. Make from Brass or mild steel. Secure inside (2) either by brazing or with retaining compound. Tap for stop rod (3)

Mild steel, rod or tube, Diameter and length to suit lathe. Coarse thread at each end.

Shortened Morse Taper to suit lathe. Tap to fit (2) and drill to clear stop rod (3)

Tap collar as per the adjusting screw

②ⓐ

1" Approx.

②

1/2"

①

soft but if not it may be necessary to use a carbide tipped drill, for the drilling. Secure a piece of rod of suitable diameter in the hole, either using retaining compound or by soft soldering. The drill will work quite well and enable a hole to be taken right through the length of the work.

The tube needs to be tapped to accept the morse taper and threaded for the tightening ring. The latter is quite a long thread to cut and the obvious answer is to screw cut and then chase the thread with a die. Very few tailstock die holders are likely to have sufficient travel to allow a die to cover the distance required. One way round this is to keep a piece of thick wall tubing with nice square ends. Put one end against the die which is held in an ordinary hand die-stock, locate the other end over a tailstock centre and use the set up to guide, not push, the die along the work. In addition a short piece of bar (part 2a) is fitted in the end of the tube and threaded for the collar, to accept the adjusting screw on the stop itself. This piece can be either

brazed or secured with a retaining compound. Although not specified as such it would be a good idea to make part 2a from bronze in order to increase the life of the tool.

Stop Adjusting Screw Part 3

The stop adjusting screw is fairly straightforward. The actual stop fits on the end and can be either brazed in to position, or it and the rod can be threaded and the stop pulled up tight so it will not move. Alternatively we can always use our old friend the retaining compound. Before fitting the stop it will be advisable to drill and tap the other end, for the retaining screw, as doing so will be very difficult if left until later.

Once again some readers may find a little difficulty in cutting the long thread. Assuming the lathe being used has screw cutting facilities, these should be used, ensuring the the job is supported at the tailstock.. Finish with a die in a hand held die holder and guided by a piece of tube as suggested above.

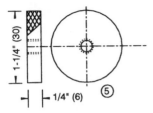

**Stop Locking Ring
locks stop rod (3)
after adjusting to
length**

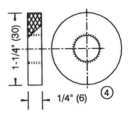

**Body Locking Ring (4)
Screws to part 2
to and pulls Morse
Taper tight.**

A square is shown on the end of the rod to accept the adjusting ring. It can be milled or filed depending on anyones particular whim. To the novice making a square can be a daunting project, however it is done. The tendency is to start with making one flat and then turning the piece round for the second, then the third. At this stage a look at the work will more often than not reveal a near perfect triangle. The opportunist will use this instead of square, no doubt, but it is not really the thing to do.

It really is not all that difficult to make a square. Simply take a short piece of square bar and thread it to fit the rod. Put a nut on the rod to act as a locking nut later. Wind the stop rod in until just the length required for the square is left protruding. But allow for the lock nut which should be done up hard and there is the perfect guide for making the square whether milled or filed. If milling, work to a figure on the mandrel and if filing count the number

of strokes for each side. The same dodge can be used for plain rod by fitting a grub screw across the square to hold the rod, and by using a hexagon bar, six sides can also be obtained

The Rings
There are three locking rings, all of which are the same except for the centre. They are shown in the first instance as plain knurled rings and as such serve their purpose very well. Anyone who wishes the job to not only be functionable but also to look smart can now seize their opportunity. All sorts of ideas come to mind, the most obvious being to machine a deep groove in the ring between outer edge and centre. They can also be painted and if done a nice bright red this has the added advantage of making them easily visible in the workshop.

Body Locking Ring Part 4
The body locking ring needs a thread to match the tube which will, depend-

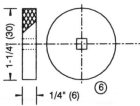

Stop Adjusting Ring Secure to (3) with screw (7). Used for adjusting length of stop

ing on the lathe be somewhere around half inch diameter. It is not at all easy to tap a piece this size with a large thread like that and so it is suggested that if possible it be screw cut at first. Then the thread can be chased out with a tap and the system makes life a lot easier that trying to tap straight away, with the tap binding and the work sliding round in the chuck. All the rings are shown as knurled, an operation which should obviously be carried out before parting off.

Parting Off
Some people will not like the idea of parting off a bar of this diameter. It should not be difficult, using the rear tool post described elsewhere in this book. Do not try and part off at high speed, remember the larger the diameter being worked on the slower the speed of the lathe revolutions. As one nears the centre of the cut, the diameter is reduced and so a higher speed

should be used. A good stout blade will be required, at least 1/8 ins. or 3mm thick and preferably 5/32 ins. or 4mm. If parting off is still found difficult, try taking two cuts. Wind the tool in for a short distance, how deep will depend on the individual. If you feel enough is enough then stop. Move the tool along the work, away from the cut by about half the width of the tool. Make another cut a little deeper than the first one. Return to the fist place and deepen the cut still more, then repeat the process above. When nearly through ensure that the final cut is at the place it is wanted and not where the relief cut is being taken or the job will end up with a nasty bump in it. In fact it is a good idea to take a shim off the back of the whole diameter as the final cut is being made, just to ensure a nice smooth finish. Always use plenty of cutting fluid when parting off steel.

If still not convinced about parting off this sort of diameter it will be necessary to resort to hack sawing. Which is good for the muscles if not necessarily the soul. Hack saws are well known for having a will of their own. Saw cuts are started with good intentions at a certain position and gradually work their way sideways until the cut looks rather like a wedge, instead of being nice and square. To avoid this make a start with a parting tool, the depth of cut need be no more than 1/8 ins. or 3mm. although if the nerve holds out go deeper. Take the work out of the lathe and saw it in the vice. Use the cut

A extended drill as may be required to make the tube. Normally the drill fits inside the extension. In this case lack of room means it must go inside

made with the parting tool as a guide and keep rotating the work between cuts so that the depth all round gradually increases, rather than sawing straight through from one side. Yet another little dodge that works quite well is to wrap a length of masking tape round the bar, ensuring that it is straight of course. Use this as a guide for the saw, once again doing a little at a time and rotating the bar in between. Once a reasonably deep cut has been established right round, it becomes possible with care to make a straight cut right through. If a hack saw is used to slice the metal then the side showing the cut will have to be faced off afterwards to make it nice and smooth.

Stop Locking Ring Part 5

Almost identical to the body locking ring except for the threaded section in the middle which in this case screws

on to the stop adjusting screw. (Part 3) The same method of construction applies. In practice, after the position of the stop has been set, the ring is screwed up hard to the rod through which the stop screw runs, thus locking it in position.

Stop Adjusting Ring Part 6

More or less the same formula as before except that a square hole is needed through the centre rather than a tapped one. Unless lucky enough to own a proper machine it will be a case of improvising. One way would be to centralise the ring in the four jaw chuck and use the slotting attachment . The jaws of the chuck can be indexed by resting a block of wood or metal on the lathe bed and pulling the jaws on to it. A special small ram and tool will need to be made if the slotting tool is to be used.

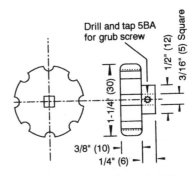

Drill and tap 5BA for grub screw
1/2" (12)
3/16" (5) Square
1-1/4" (30)
3/8" (10)
1/4" (6)

Eight Semi Circular grooves 5/32"
4mm radii. Extend square section
of part 3 to suit to a length of 1/2 " (12)

Alternative Adjusting Ring

USEFUL WORKSHOP TOOLS

If the square is going to be filed to shape we can make life easy for ourselves by doing a bit of careful marking out and drilling. Start with a small centre and then draw the square round it, the dashed lines in the drawings show this. Draw diagonal lines to each corner and make a tiny centre pop along each. The mark to be at a distance which will allow a small hole to be drilled that will just barely touch the edge of the square. drill holes in all four places. In the case of a 3/16" square the distance down the diagonal will be 1/16 ins. and the holes 3/32 ins. diameter. Whatever happens, even if it means drilling slightly undersize. do not let the edge of the holes go outside the square. Finally return the work to the lathe using the four jaw chuck, and carefully centre it by lining up with the original centre pop. Drill and finish to size a hole of the diameter that the square is going to be. It is now a very simple job to ease the rest of the metal out with a needle file and to finish with a really square hole.

Alternative Wheels

Finally for those that do not like the idea of the knurled wheels, or perhaps feel that they do not give sufficient grip an alternative design is offered for the adjuster. The others can be replaced with hexagon nuts. It has finger grooves which can either be made with a bull nose end mill, or a plain end mill can be used and the grooves rounded off. If indexing is a problem use the method shown for the square but with a piece of hexagon material instead. It does mean of course six grooves instead of eight, which is not quite as comfortable but it will still do the job. These wheels should be rounded off at the edges by about 3/32 ins. or 2.5mm rather than left square in order to avoid the possibility of cutting ones hands.The grooves should also be rounded off at the edges for the same reason.

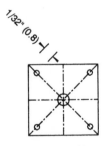

Mark diagonals on square. Measure 1.32" (0.8) down diagonal.

Drill holes 3/64" (1.2mm) on each diagonal

Drill 5/32" (4mm) to break into previously drilled holes. File out rest of metal

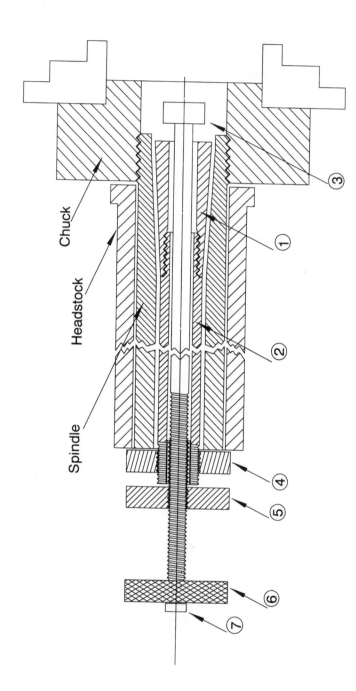

Chuck

Headstock

Spindle

① ② ③ ④ ⑤ ⑥ ⑦

Sectioned View of stop, showing assembly.

Rear Mounted Tool Posts

The photograph shows a simple type of rear tool post with a small extension. It will work quite well and is very easy to construct. There is no reason why in order to simplify construction further it should not have a simple slot for the tool holder, rather than the screw adjustable one shown.

Most lathes do not come with a rear tool post and in fact on nearly all, the fitting of such a device creates problems due to lack of space. This is a shame as the rear tool post is a very handy item, particularly when parting off. If a parting tool is used in the normal position the thrust created is towards the top of the lathe bearings and if there is any play, the work will tend to lift and ride up on the tool. The can have two effects; it may very well snap the tool or alternatively the tool will dig into the work and seize up the lathe. In doing so there is every chance the work will be damaged beyond repair.

Advantages

By mounting our tool to the rear the pressure is applied in a downward direction and the two effects referred to above become far less likely to occur. This is not to say that mishaps cannot happen and with worn bearings or a badly adjusted cross slide they still might. The results are usually much less of a disaster. The tool of course is mounted in the rear tool post facing in the opposite direction to usual or perhaps we should say upside down.

Working in this fashion does not mean we can ignore the usual rules for lathe work. The tool must be sharp and

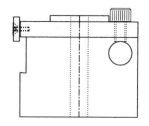
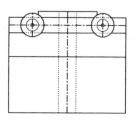

Tool Post for holding parting tool blade, Machine narrow slot, a good fit for the width of blade and slightly narrower than blade thickness. Include a 1 degree taper at bottom as shown. Secure blade in position with thick washers and c/sunk screws.

Alternative type of tool post. Use the same sizes but machine narrow slot for parting tool blade and hole to fit a boring bar. Check that both will bring cutting edge of tool to centre height.

well honed as well as tightened hard down in the tool post. A good cutting fluid should be used.

The rear tool post need not just be used for parting off. It is useful if a second machining operation is required without moving the normal cutting tool. In this respect the added rigidity is an advantage when using a form tool. It is also possible to get very good finishes by boring from the rear. Again the added rigidity is an advantage by reducing chatter and vibration.

The Need for Support

having established that for many purposes, the most important of which is parting off, the rear tool has considerable advantages. We now come to the question of space. In any form of lathe work, the more rigidly tools can be held the better they will work. If not well supported there is a tenancy for a vibrating or perhaps we could call it a bouncing action to be set up. With normal turning operations the end result is chatter and an uneven surface imparted to the finish work. The same

will apply when working from the other side of the lathe. Our rear mounted tool post therefore must be a rigid construction and as large as practical.

Finding Room

Making the tool post rigid also means making it heavy and as a piece of steel or cast iron is a given weight for a given size, it follows that it should be as large as practical. That is a very fine theory but in making it large we also take up space and many lathes have quite a limited size to their cross slides. It is true that on some it is possible to buy a longer cross slide than normal, which the manufacturers make more or less specifically for the purpose we have in mind. In many instances however this is not possible or perhaps not desirable and so to mount a rear tool post opposite the normal one means that space in between the tools is extremely limited.

The normal practice to cope with the situation is to make a small bolt -on extension and put the new tool post on that. The idea is simple enough, make

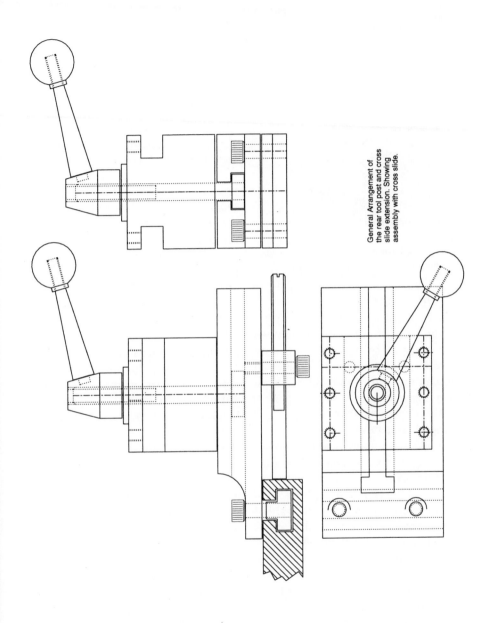

General Arrangement of the rear tool post and cross slide extension. Showing assembly with cross slide.

The improved design rear toolpost, support underneath allows extra overhang so that the tool post can be pulled out of the way. It also allows the use of a heavier tool post which gives greater rigidity.

the new post of a suitable height so that a hefty piece of mild steel plate can be fixed underneath it, which will overhang the end of the slide and the problem is solved.

A simple Tool Post
to actually make a tool post is simplicity in itself. All that is needed is a suitable block of mild steel, or cast iron, cut a slot in the side to accept the parting tool, a couple of screw holes, for the bolts that will hold the tool in position and another hole to bolt down the post to the extension. It is the sort of job that the average model engineer can cope with in an odd hour or so. The extension must not overhang the cross slide by more than a couple of

inches at the most and the extension piece is secured with a single tee bolt. The extension should be of mild steel, rather than cast iron which might just possibly be a little bit brittle for this sort of work.

Making Improvements
While the foregoing idea works quite well it is still not an ideal solution and space is still limited, making it difficult to measure work with a micrometer. The answer of course is to remove the rear post and put it back every time we are proposing to part off, but this is to say the least extremely tedious. A longer extension is therefore the answer, the question being. How to make one without putting undue strain on the lathe?

An Improved Design
The design that follows does this by the simple expedient of supporting the extension from the back and also allows a much larger and therefore more rigid tool post to be incorporated.
Part 1 The Slide Extension
The extension is made from a really hefty piece of mild steel plate but is not at all difficult to make. Start by squaring the ends of the plate, as bought from a stockist, the chances are that these will be sawn rather than machined and will not only, not be square but the finish will probably not be of a very high quality. With that done mill a slot down the centre as a start to making the tee slot. Making the

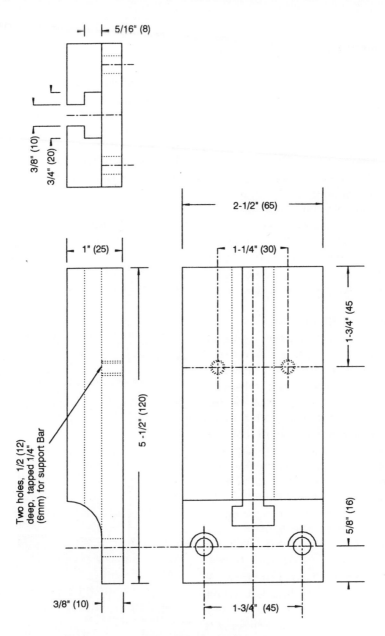

5/16" (8)

3/8" (10)

3/4" (20)

2-1/2" (65)

1" (25)

1-1/4" (30)

1-3/4" (45)

5 -1/2" (120)

Two holes, 1/2 (12) deep, tapped 1/4" (6mm) for support Bar

3/8" (10)

5/8" (16)

1-3/4" (45)

Part Number 1 Cross Slide Extension from Mild Steel.

actual tee section calls for a special cutter, in theory. In practice it can be done with a tool rather like a fly-cutter but with the cutting tool coming from the side rather than the bottom edge. Alternatively it is not that difficult to make a reasonable properly shaped cutter. This can be made as a single item from a piece of silver steel. There is no suggestion it will be as efficient as a proper tee slot cutter but it will save the expense of buying one for what will probably be a one off job.Over the years many of these tools made as a one off, if kept will be found suitable for something else later on.

Cutter From Silver Steel

For the size of slot required for the job a piece of 3/4 ins.. diameter silver steel will be required, about four inches in length. Silver steel of such a diameter is expensive but nowhere near as costly as it would be to buy a cutter. Turn a length to 3/8 ins. or 10mm diameter for the shank. Quite what length is required, will depend entirely on the machine and cutter holder to be used, generally about three inches will be long enough. Put a centre in the end of the machined section and thread it twenty threads to the inch or 1mm pitch if working in metric.. That is assuming that the type of cutter holder is in use that accepts threaded cutters. Some rely on other methods of retention and the shank of the home made cutter must be adjusted accordingly.

With the shank finished, machine a

piece of the full diameter material to 5/16 ins. or 8mm in length. It is now a question of cutting the teeth to convert the blank into our tee slot cutter. Anyone who is chicken hearted can opt for a single cutting edge and as long as the work is done slowly it will do the job quite well. Braver hearts will no doubt be willing to make three cutting edges.

The Cutting Edges

making the cutting edges is not as difficult as it may sound. Mark of three divisions and saw and file them to shape. They do not all have to be iden-

The underside of the toolpost extension, showing the tee bar and support bars. These show an addition to the layout on the drawings as a knurled collar has been fitted to each to assist in adjustment. They were secured with retaining compound. After adjustment the lock nuts must be tightened up.

USEFUL WORKSHOP TOOLS

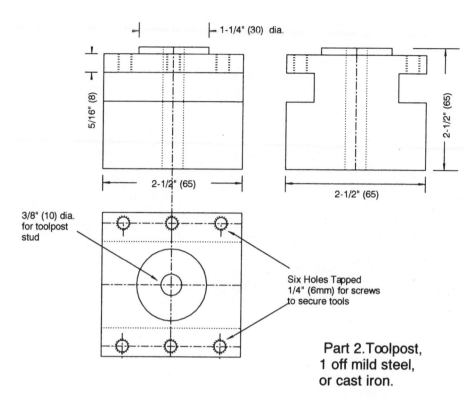

‑| |‑ 1-1/4" (30) dia.

5/16" (8)

2-1/2" (65)

2-1/2" (65)

2-1/2" (65)

3/8" (10) dia.
for toolpost
stud

Six Holes Tapped
1/4" (6mm) for screws
to secure tools

**Part 2. Toolpost,
1 off mild steel,
or cast iron.**

tical, although it is better if they are. But it is important that the actual cutting edges are all at the same diameter. Otherwise you might just as well have made a single cutting edge in the first place. To prevent reducing the diameter of the edges it is suggested that instead of a straight edge it is left round. In theory this does not give the correct angle for cutting, but in practice the idea works quite well. The cutting edge is recommended as ten degrees and trying to file a ten degree flat invariably seems to result in a reduction of the overall diameter of the tool. With the flutes completed polish

the edges as much as possible and then harden and temper to a light straw colour. Hey Presto! one tee slot cutter.

Getting back to the extension, having we hope successfully cut the tee slot there are now four holes to be drilled. Two are clearance holes to accept the Allen Screws that secure the piece to the cross slide. The other two are tapped to accept the bolts that hold the support bar in position. The front of the extension is cut away and is shown as rounded off. This is purely cosmetic and a straightforward ninety degree cut would do just as well. The

The tool post in operation, showing how the tool is pressing down against the most rigid part of the lathe. In this instance the parting tool is being used to machine a groove in a component.

cut out section makes more room when making adjustments and shorter screws are needed to hold the piece in position.

If the curvature is adopted it will be found that the surface that the heads of the Allen Screws will rest on is not flat. A slight counterbore might be required which will just break into the curved section. Again this is indicated on the drawing.

Part 2 Tool posts

Two variations of tool post are shown on the drawings, in fact it is possible to make any type to suit individual needs. Construction of these is straightforward enough. The central hole should be drilled while the metal is held in the four jaw chuck. Milling the slots speaks for itself, as does the task of drilling and tapping the holes for the screws to hold the tools in position.

The first type of tool post, as can be seen in the photographs is designed to accept a complete parting tool holder and has two slots in order to make it a little more versatile. If two different sizes of tool holders are available there is no reason why the slots should not be made different sizes to accommodate them. The most important factor is that when the parting tool is set in the tool post, the cutting edge must be at the exact centre height of the mandrel. Adjustments can be made with the aid of shims.

USEFUL WORKSHOP TOOLS

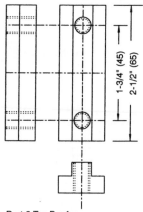

1-3/4" (45)
2-1/2" (65)

Part 3 Tee Bar for
fixing extension
to cross slide.
Material, mild steel
all dimensions to
suit individual lathe
except those shown

The second version is designed to accept the parting tool blade directly into the holder, a method which many prefer. It should mean that there will be less vibration as another possible source, the tool holder, has been eliminated. The slot for the blade is made slightly narrower than the blade itself, but we are talking of only a minute amount here. It is secured to the tool post with countersunk screws set into thick washers. generally parting tool blades have an angle ground along one edge, usually around ten degrees but it may pay to check to make sure. A matching angle has to be machined in the tool post and here again a home made cutter will do the job very well. A single cutting edge, giving a fly cutting type of operation is all that is needed and the diameter of the silver steel used for the cutter can be considerable less than that used for making the tee slots.

The other side of that tool post is shown with a round hole to take a boring bar. Boring is another operation that tends to create vibration, due to the need to use a comparatively thin tool to fit in the hole. Once again cutting while the tool is pushing downward can help to alleviate this effect. Do remember however to put the tool in upside down, something which it is all too easy to forget. It also of course needs to be at centre height.

Part 3 Tee Bar

Tee bar sounds almost like an excuse for a break but it is in fact more or less two tee pieces stuck together. Not literally that is, as it is made from one piece. The holes must of course match those in the extension piece, and the bar itself should be a good fit in the cross slide tee slots. It pays to run a file along the edges after machining as a good sliding fit is essential. If left as machined, small pieces of swarf tend to work their way in and cause the bar to stick in the slots. A nice smooth finish will allow it to slide in and out freely while not having any excessive

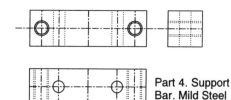

Part 4. Support
Bar. Mild Steel

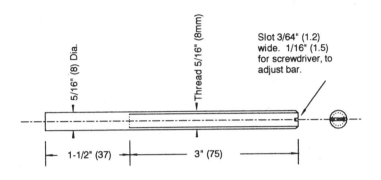

5/16" (8) Dia.

Thread 5/16" (8mm)

Slot 3/64" (1.2) wide. 1/16" (1.5) for screwdriver, to adjust bar.

1-1/2" (37)

3" (75)

Part 5 Support Rods (Two Off)

play. Very slightly chamfering the edges also helps to get free movement,

Part 4 The Support Bar

Support bar is just a name for a piece of square mild steel with four holes drilled in it. Two are clearance size while the other two are tapped for the support rods. It is important off course that all holes should be drilled square but it is extra important for the tapped ones for the support rods.

Part 5 Support Rods

The support rods are adjusted to push against the cross slide and so put sufficient tension on to prevent any chance of it twisting during operations. They are nothing more complicated than pieces of mild steel that have been threaded at one end which also has a slot cut in it to allow a screwdriver to be used to make adjustments. A nut is put on behind the support bar and tightened to act as a locking device after adjustment. The rods should be tight-ened right up after the extension piece has been located and need to be adjust-ed every time the assembly is put back after being removed from the lathe.

Part 6 Tee Bolt

The tee bolt which both secures and allows adjustment of the tool post is best fabricated. Like the support bars it is simply a case of threading a piece of rod to a suitable size. The difference is that on one end a strip of bar is used to act as the tee. This can be secured to the bolt either by brazing it in position or by tapping it and screwing the rod to it. In the latter case a retaining com-pound should be used to secure it in position. Once again ensure that it is a good running fit in the tee slot, with as little shake as possible.

Part 7 The Handle

Start by machining the main part. The taper on the top is about fifteen degrees and can easily be made by setting the top slide over.The tapered rod that acts as a lever, is reduced at each end to a parallel section. The section that is fitted with a plastic ball handle is threaded for that. Sometimes these handles have rather larger threads than are practical for model engineering purposes, in which case an adaptor will have to be made.

The other end is silver soldered into the main section. Should the idea of silver soldering such a piece not appeal, both parts could be threaded and secured with retaining compound. It may be found that in use it is best if a thin washer is interposed between the handle and the tool post. This will allow easier adjustment as well as better security.

Usage

Use of the set up is fairly obvious. The tool post can be slid in and out towards the chuck as one wishes. If space is required around the chuck it can be pushed right out the way. If this is done, also turn the post round so that the cutting edge of the tool is facing away from the operator, thus providing a measure of safety from cuts, etc. It may well be found that in practice the device is versatile enough to leave in situ for most of the time and rarely will need be to be taken off. In which case from time to time check the tension on the support rods, to ensure they have not become slack.

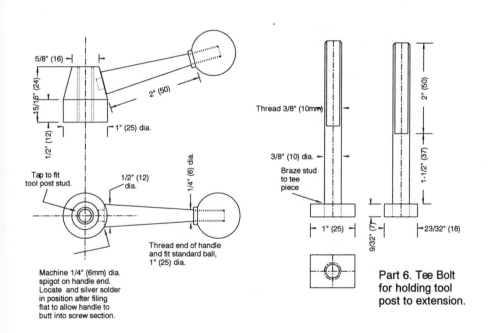

5/8" (16)

15/16" (24)

1/2" (12)

2" (50)

1" (25) dia.

Tap to fit tool post stud.

1/2" (12) dia.

1/4" (6) dia.

Thread end of handle and fit standard ball, 1" (25) dia.

Machine 1/4" (6mm) dia. spigot on handle end. Locate and silver solder in position after filing flat to allow handle to butt into screw section.

Thread 3/8" (10mm)

3/8" (10) dia.

Braze stud to tee piece

1" (25)

9/32" (7)

2" (50)

1-1/2" (37)

23/32" (18)

Part 6. Tee Bolt for holding tool post to extension.

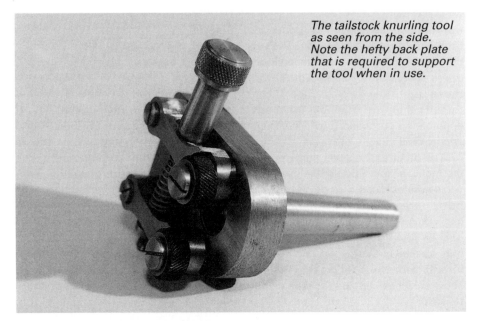

The tailstock knurling tool as seen from the side. Note the hefty back plate that is required to support the tool when in use.

A Tailstock Mounted Knurling Tool

Knurling is an operation which is often carried out by the model engineer. There are all sorts of cases where it is necessary to knurl a piece of work, the most frequent is when making tools and we need a handle or some form of adjuster on which it is necessary to get a good grip. It is a process also used quite often in model making, hand-wheels and other fittings are knurls, both for the sake of appearance and to enable us to grip them better. It follows therefore that knurling tools are an essential part of the model engineers' equipment.

Types of Knurling Tools

Over the years there have been numerous knurling tools described in the model engineering press, be it magazines or books and they take a variety of forms. The simplest is a tool with a single knurling wheel, but while this is very easy to make it is not the best type for the home workshop. The lathes we use are lighter than those generally found in industry and using the single wheel tool imparts a great deal of sideways strain on the bearings. Constant use of such a tool could therefore in the long run irreparably

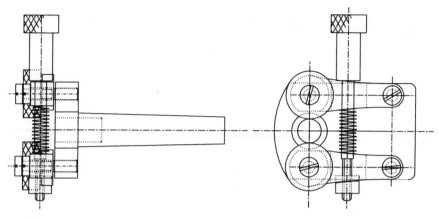

Front and End view of the tailstock knurling tool

damage the machine. At the same time for very light work on softer materials such a tool does have its place and can be very useful.

Calliper Tools

The calliper type tool works by applying pressure to top and bottom of the work, thus taking most of the strain from the bearings. A number of different tools have been designed on this principle and have been very successful. Once again though there is a difficulty with them in certain circumstances. They are held in the toolpost, so unless an indexable holder is available their use involves removing the cutting tool and replacing it with the knurling tool. If a single item is being made this probably matters little. but if two or more the same are wanted the difficulty arises of getting the cutting tool set back to the exact position required.

If quick change tool holders are in use a knurling tool can be made to fit them and the cutting tools can then be returned to their correct position, It means that the knurling tool will have to be lightly constructed and by their very nature this is against all principles of the operation.

Knurling involves mainly forcing metal to a shape, using pressure, rather than a cutting action. The wheels dig into the metal and the pressure indents the pattern of the wheel which is invariably harder than the metal being worked on. In fact the action actually raises the metal around the pattern making the area a slightly larger diameter than it was originally.

Tailstock Knurling

The principle behind a tailstock mounted tool is identical to that of the calliper, The difference being that by supporting the tool in the tailstock we can

Having lined the top slide angle up as accurately as possible by using flat metal bar, check it for accuracy with a clock gauge. Sometimes a home made taper will be inclined to slip no matter how accurate we believe it to be This can often be cured by machining a shallow groove in the centre, leaving about 1ins. or 25mm each end.

keep the toolpost free to hold the cutting tool. Thus if more than one item is needed stops can be set for the cutting tool, allowing repeat operations to be carried out.

At first glance this type of tool looks much more complicated than the normal calliper. In fact, the only slightly difficult part being the machining of the taper to fit the tailstock. The rest of the tool follows exactly the same system as the calliper, with one minor difference. A backplate is needed on which to mount the arms.

The tool that is about to be described will accept knurling wheels up to an inch in diameter and 3/8 ins. thick. other sizes can of course be used but to do so it will be necessary to modify the length and possibly the diameter of the pins.

Machining The Taper

Assuming a top slide is available that can be set at an angle, there is no need whatever to panic about machining the taper. All sorts of suggestions are made as to how it should be done,

USEFUL WORKSHOP TOOLS

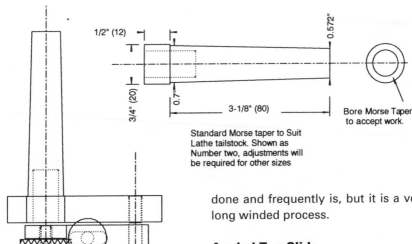

1/2" (12)

0.572"

3/4" (20)

0.7"

3-1/8" (80)

Bore Morse Taper to accept work.

Standard Morse taper to Suit Lathe tailstock. Shown as Number two, adjustments will be required for other sizes

Plan View of Assembled Knurling Tool

done and frequently is, but it is a very long winded process.

Angled Top Slide.

To use the top slide put a piece of round bar in the three jaw chuck and put a centre in it. Use a small centre drill as it does not need to be very deep. Put a centre in the tailstock and support another between the piece in the chuck and the tailstock. Some lathe centres do not have holes in the rear but most do, make sure the one used is centred.

Put a piece of square bar in the toolpost, checking that it is exactly ninety degrees to the chuck face. Loosen the top slide and turn it round so that the bar in the tool post lies flush along the suspended centre.To make sure check with feeler gauges to ensure there are no gaps at one end. Remove the bar and mount a clock gauge on the cross slide in such a way that the indicator is touching the suspended centre. Wind the top slide backwards and forwards and see if there is any discrepancy on the

from using a proper taper turning attachment, to setting over the tailstock to get the required angle.

Setting the tailstock over is really fraught with danger. It is achieved by undoing a screw at the base and pushing the top section across the bed. To turn a taper this way requires the tailstock to be set at exactly the right distance across. To get this right depends on the length of the material which has to be set between centres. If it is a fraction over the calculated length then the taper will be wrong. How does one calculate exactly the length required anyway? Certain other factors come into play here. The work using this method must be machined between centres and this means that to get the exact length the centres in the work have to be very precise. It can of course be gauge. If it is set at zero at one end of the taper it should still be at zero when the top slide gets to the other end. It may be necessary to make some final adjustments. When it is correct the top slide is set perfectly to turn the taper.

Making a Start

Having set the top slide over it is time to make a start on the machining. Start with a bar of suitable size but over length. Three quarters of an inch or twenty millimetres is about right for a two Morse Taper, a piece of one inch or twenty four millimetres will be needed for a number three. Owners of the miniature lathes will need to check for themselves as sometimes odd sizes like one and a half, are used on these machines. Put a centre in one end to support it with the tailstock and mount it in a three jaw chuck. It is now possible to machine the taper to size. Use callipers to check the large and small end sizes, using a known taper as reference. Make sure that a sharp tool is used and

A front view of the knurling tool, showing quite clearly the arms, pivot, spring, etc. Note also the hole in the body that allows smaller diameter work to pas through.

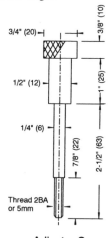

Front Plate-One off mild Steel

Bore 3/4" or 20mm
Tap 0BA or 6mm
1/8" radius
3" (76)
3/4" (20) 1/2" (12)
1/4" (6)
1/2" (12)
1-1/2" (38)
1/4" (6)

Adjuster Screw

3/4" (20)
3/8" (10)
1/2" (12)
1" (25)
1/4" (6)
7/8" (22)
2-1/2" (63)
Thread 2BA or 5mm

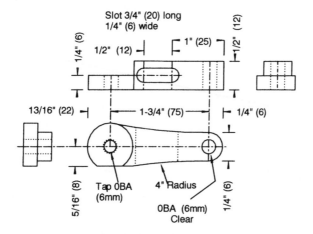

Slot 3/4" (20) long
1/4" (6) wide

1/4" (6)

1/2" (12)

1" (25)

1/2" (12)

13/16" (22)

1-3/4" (75)

1/4" (6)

5/16" (8)

Tap 0BA
(6mm)

4" Radius

0BA (6mm)
Clear

1/4" (6)

Arms:- two off - mild steel
Left & right handed
ends 13/32" - 11mm
and 1/8"-6mm radius
Remove 1/16" (1.5) on larger
radius to allow clearance for
knurling wheel.

try and ensure as good a finish as possible on the final cuts. It is worth while checking that there is no play on the top slide before commencing work.

With the taper finished, put it in the headstock and drill or bore the recess which allows clearance of the work being knurled. Some readers may find they have a larger taper in the lathe headstock than in the tailstock. If so put the new taper in the tailstock and centre drill and drill the component from the headstock using the three jaw chuck, It does mean that it will not be possible to bore the recess and drilling will have to be relied

upon, resulting probably in a finish that is not as good as one might like. It may be possible to turn the taper round and hold the non tapered section in the chuck and finish the work with a boring bar.

The Body

This is just a name given to a piece of flat plate for the sake of something better to call it. and it consists of nothing more than a piece of plate with three holes in it.The drawings show it as slightly shaped and while this is a good idea in order to save fingers being cut on sharp corners it is not essential

The large hole will have to be bored to size and it must be a good fit on the taper section. It can be made a press fit by machining it the tiniest bit smaller in diameter than the flat section of the Morse Taper. Alternatively machine it about the same amount oversize and secure it with a retaining compound. The third alternative being to pin it in position.

It must fit at exactly ninety degree to the taper otherwise the knurling will not be accurate. Do not therefore if the press fit method is chosen try and hammer the parts together. Put them in a vice and gradually squeeze them until the body is correctly located on the taper. The same method of location can be used to ensure accuracy if either of the other methods of joining the parts are chosen.

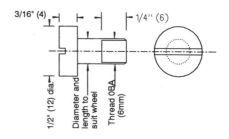

Pins for Knurling Wheels
Two off from Silver Steel
Length to suit wheels
Cut 1/16" (1.5) x 1/16" (1.5) slots. Harden, temper light straw.

The Arms

The arms are again straight forward enough although care must be taken to ensure that the holes match each other. One end has clearance holes for the pins that will hold the arms to the body, the other is tapped for the pins holding the knurling wheels. That end is also reduced in diameter to allow the knurling wheel to nestle in and locate as close as possible to the support supplied by the taper and body.

Knurl Pins

Almost identical to the arm pins the length must depend on the width of the knurling wheels that are being used. The threaded section fits in the arm rather than in the body and the pins which are made from silver steel and hardened, with a very light straw temper. This hardening process is essential as if the pins are not sufficiently hard they will snap first time the tool is used. The hardness must nearly match that of the wheels, although getting it exactly right is probably not possible in the home workshop. Should readers have any doubts about their ability to harden the pins then they should be made of a good quality bronze. In which case they will not break when used.

Adjusting Screw

A reasonably straight forward turning job the screw can be made in two ways. Either completely machined from a solid bar or fabricated. In the latter case make the top section drilling and tapping the end to accept the spigot, which after threading for the nut is held in place with retaining compound. Make sure the thread is a good full one as a lot of pressure will be applied to it when the tool is tightened up.

The Nut

The nut is a little bit of an odd ball as in order for it to fit nicely in the lower arm it has a semi-circular piece filed in the top. It should be threaded first and then filed to shape. The actual radius of the curved section is not important. While it would be very nice to have a perfect fit with the curve on the arm it is very unlikely that most people will be able to attain this and in fact almost any radii slightly smaller that that in the arm, will do the trick.

The Spring

Most people will almost certainly use any odd spring of a suitable size that comes to hand. In theory it should be of twenty gauge or 1mm diameter wire with an inner core of 1/4 ins. or 6mm. But that hardly matters as long as it is not so strong that the tool cannot be closed up.

Operation

The knurling tool is used in exactly the same way as any other similar tool. The wheels are closed on the work and just tightened a little. The lathe is rotated at a very slow speed and the tool moved along to cover the required distance. Without removing it tighten it and move it back slowly and continue in this manner until it is thought that the knurl created is satisfactory. Use plenty of cutting oil which will help to obtain a good finish.

Sometimes it pays to rotate the lathe by hand when starting the knurling process as this gives greater control. The mandrel handle described elsewhere is ideal for this purpose.

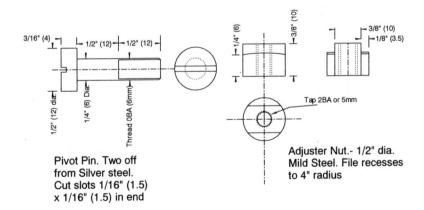

Pivot Pin. Two off
from Silver steel.
Cut slots 1/16" (1.5)
x 1/16" (1.5) in end

Tap 2BA or 5mm

Adjuster Nut.- 1/2" dia.
Mild Steel. File recesses
to 4" radius

The photograph shows the completed self releasing handle. It is a most useful addition to the lathe and will greatly expand its versatility.

Self Releasing Mandrel Handle

There are a number of instances where it is desirable to rotate the lathe by hand. The most obvious one is when tapping with the tap in the tailstock, the same applies to threading with a die. It can also be useful when screw cutting and a start can be made and then power applied when it becomes obvious that the work is going well. Setting up work is yet another example and we could probably go on thinking of them.

In order to rotate the machine by hand we usually have to pull it round via the chuck, or perhaps the drive belts. There are two main objections to the former idea. Firstly if the chuck is screwed to the mandrel there is a chance that it might come undone as it is pulled. Secondly, when pulling on the chuck we are also pulling against the gearing provided by the drive belts, unless they are disconnected. This brings us to the second method which is to use the drive belts themselves. They are awkward to hold and pulling them round is a very messy business as during normal operations they pick up all sorts of dirt and grease. Neither method allows a nice smooth rotation but involves constant stopping and starting as the hands continually need to be relocated. The answer therefore is a handle.

Making a handle is quite straightforward all that is required is some form of device to lock a piece of rod to the mandrel itself and attach a handle to it. The locking device can be a cone into a split tube, which when pulled tight with a screw expands the tube ends hard into the bore, with the result that any rotational movement of the screw also rotates the mandrel.

The system work perfectly and a simple handle added to the screw will do the job perfectly well. It must be removed when the lathe is put under power as if not it will rotate with it. Handles generally being lop sided affairs the end result of switching the lathe on with one held in it is a severe vibration that shakes the whole machine and certainly prevents any work being done on it. A way round this of course would be to make a double sided handle so that if the lathe was accidentally switched on with it in position it would balance itself and there would be little if any vibration. Unfortunately the double sided handle in itself, is awkward to use, being difficult to rotate without the second handle section getting in the way. So it is not the complete answer.

The Self Releasing Handle

The way to solve all the problems referred to above is to make the handle capable of releasing itself so that it is not possible to leave it in position accidentally. To do this a spring is fitted that pushes the handle away once pressure is released and that is exactly the way this device works. In order to turn the lathe by hand the handle is pushed slightly forward to engage it

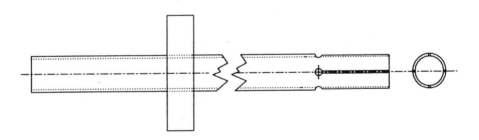

Tubing, diameter to fit lathe. Length approximately 9-1/2".
Braze on stop collar. 1-1/2" from end drill four 1/8" diameter
holes round periphery. cut 1/32" wide slots to tube end.

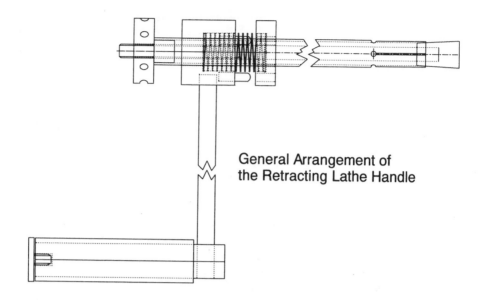

General Arrangement of
the Retracting Lathe Handle

and as soon as it is released it disen-
gages itself. This does not mean to
say that it should be left attached all
the time if only because while it is in
position it is not possible to pass stock
right through the mandrel. It is useful
where work requires a machining
operation or two and possibly threading, it is also ideal for setting work and
then switching on the machine to
check that the setting is accurate,
without having to bother to remove
the handle.

The device has to be tailored entirely to a particular lathe and so in the
description and drawings that follow,
measurements are most definitely
there as a guide only. They are
Imperial because the design originally
was for a British Lathe and it is not

practical to give metric conversions
unless they can relate to a particular
lathe. There is sufficient information
to allow a handle to be built to fit any
lathe with a hollow mandrel, by anyone, whether experienced or a novice.

The Expanding Tube
The tube in which the cone slides
should be thin walled and a nice sliding fit in the mandrel bore. If there is
too much side play the cone will not
open it enough to lock it in position.
Equally if the tube is too thick it will be
difficult to open the ends and either
will not work at all, or a excessive
force will be needed. The tube in the
drawings is forty thousandths of an
inch or about 1mm thick. The length
as shown is designed to take it well

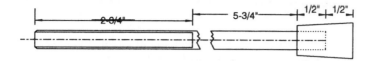

| 2-3/4" | 5-3/4" | 1/2" | 1/2" |

The Expander. Make from Mild Steel

into the mandrel and give a lot of support. It could be shortened by about one third and no harm done.

Whether or not a suitable piece of tubing is available will be largely a matter of luck. It may be necessary for some people to use solid bar and bore it out. If that is so there is no point in attempting to bore the whole length full diameter. About a couple of inches will be plenty long enough and will give plenty of opportunity for expansion. The rest of it can be drilled clearance size for the thread. All that is, except for a short length at the other end, which will need to be tapped to the size of whatever thread is to be used.

It will be seen from the drawings that where a piece of tubing has been used the end to which we are referring is closed down with a short length of bar threaded as described above. This piece will need to be silver soldered in position, or alternatively it could be held with three screws. If screws are chosen it will be necessary to leave the fitting of this part until later in the assembly as the handle unit will pass along the tube and the screws would be in the way.

A little way from the open end of the

tube drill four holes spaced equally around the periphery. Connect these to the end with thin slots. These are best made with a slitting saw but a junior hacksaw could be used if a slitting saw is not available. Don't be tempted to make the slots too wide, nothing will be gained by so doing and the greater the area that will come into contact with the mandrel bore, the better.

Fitted to the tube a short way from the closed end is a short length of large diameter steel bar. This is one side of the dog clutch and also acts as a support for the spring. It has three holes that match the pins in the other side of the clutch and there is a recess bored for the spring to fit into. Basically a straight forward lathe oper-

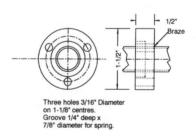

Three holes 3/16" Diameter
on 1-1/8" centres.
Groove 1/4" deep x
7/8" diameter for spring.

Scrap view of part of clutch attached to tube

ation the only part that some people might find a little tricky is drilling the three holes. They can be indexed by using the three chuck jaws locating on a piece of hardwood resting on the lathe bed. Marking the positions can be done with a centre punch mounted in the tool post.

If marking the other side of the clutch is likely to create problems a simple way will be revealed later. In the meantime, go head and drill right through the piece, but do make sure the holes are at ninety degrees to the face, otherwise problems will arise later. The counterbore for the spring is quite straight forward.

Cone and Thread

The cone is made from a short length of mild steel rod, the outside diameter of which is the same as the outside diameter of the tube. Take a length of bar and start by drilling and tapping the thread. Next machine the taper using the top slide set to an angle of about three degrees. While not absolutely critical, if the taper is too steep it will not easily open the tube. At the same time if it is too shallow it will not fit in the bore unless made longer than the drawings specify. Finally part off and the cone is ready for use.

The thread or perhaps threaded rod can be a piece of studding, alternatively a length of round bar can be threaded at each end. The end that fits in to the cone must be locked up as tight as

possible or even secured with an adhesive. An alternative would be to make the thread a little longer and fit a lock nut. Whatever happens we do not want it coming undone, particularly when the cone is pulled up tight.

Handle and Dog Clutch

we will start with the dog clutch which is a piece of round bar of the same diameter as that fitted over the tube. It is bored to allow the threaded rod to pass through and counterbored for the spring to recess into it. In addition it holds three pins which will locate into the other half of the clutch. Careful indexing is called for to get these to line up exactly with the holes. There is an alternative, that is to take a short length of round bar of the same diameter as the recesses in both sides of the clutch and a little shorter than the sum of the depth of the two holes combined. Use this as a guide to hold the two pieces together and pass the drill through one of the holes in the piece that will be secured to the tube. Take it full depth into the second piece, then separate the parts and fit a pin.

No mention has been made so far of how the pins will be secured. Threading is the most obvious way with the use of an adhesive as the next obvious suggestion. Before fitting the pin make sure the end is rounded off as this will help when locating the clutch. With one pin secure and the piece of bar acting as a guide it is now easy to pass the drill through and drill the other two holes and they should line up without any bother. That of course is always assuming that the division into three parts has been accurate in the first place. If not the clutch will only locate in one position instead of three.

Anyone with a mind and the expertise to do so can increase the number of pins and holes. Six would be a highly desirable number as then the handle will only need to move sixty degrees to locate with the other part, instead of a hundred and twenty as it will be with three pins. This must be a matter of individual choice, if six is the figure chosen, it will be of no advantage if even one of the holes does not line up correctly. It will then mean a three hundred and sixty degree rotation to engage the clutch, it is easier to get three properly located than six.

The handle is made in two parts. Firstly a piece of round stock, which is secured in the clutch at ninety degrees. It can again be either threaded or possibly brazed, depending on individual choice. This in turn is set at ninety degrees in another piece of bar and secured, again the choice of how being up to the individual. Before fitting it drill and tap the end and make large headed screw to fit the tapped hole. The screw stops a piece of plastic tube which is fitted over the bar from coming off, while allowing it to rotate.

Tightening Ring

The final part is the tightening ring which fits on the screw and behind the clutch. When done up it pushes against the tube end and pulls the cone tightly into the tube, locking it to the mandrel. The ring is shown as having a series of holes round the outside, these are for fitting a small tommy bar in order to get plenty of leverage. Although it would not look so good this ring can be replaced with an ordinary nut which will do the job just as well.

The Spring

The final part required is a light spring one and half inches diameter, seven eighths of an inch outside diameter and ten turns to the inch. Made of twenty gauge spring wire it can easily be made on the lathe. It must be confessed that the one in the original handle was not home made but came out of a cycle pump. It was a very old pump possibly from one of the really old fashioned cycles and it is probable that the spring from a modern pump may be of a different size.

That then is the manufacture of a spring loaded handle. When fitted to the lathe in normal operation the handle drops to its lowest point and remains there while the lathe is running. To use it, when the lathe is stopped of course, simple push it forward until the clutch engages and then rotate it as required.

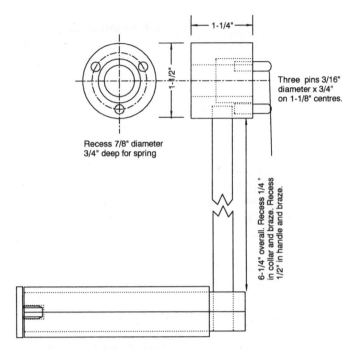

|← 1-1/4" →|

1-1/2"

Three pins 3/16"
diameter x 3/4"
on 1-1/8" centres.

Recess 7/8" diameter
3/4" deep for spring

6-1/4" overall. Recess 1/4 "
in collar and braze. Recess
1/2" in handle and braze.

Handle from 3/4" diameter mild steel. 4" long.
Cross drill one end for down rod tap other
2 BA for large headed screw. Fit plastic tube
(electrical conduit)over rod and retaining screw.

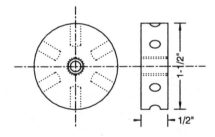

1-1/2"

|← 1/2" →|

Six holes in rim, 3/16" diameter
by 3/8" deep. Tap centre hole
to accept tightening screw

Nut for drawing cone tight
one off from mild steel

x

An Improved Milling Vice

The completed vice of unusual design.

There have been a number of machine vices described in various publications, but this one is a little different in as much as the moving jaw tightens with the main pressure at the top. Most of which work via a lead screw which is usually, for the sake of convenience of construction set fairly low down. This means that the push imparted by the screw is at the base of the moving jaw allowing some movement of the top, with the result that the bottom of the jaw receives the greater torque. The better the quality of the vice the less the tendency to do this as there are devices built in aimed at stopping such movement, mostly they consist of a plate at the bottom of the moving jaw which runs in a recess in the base of the vice, the longer this piece is, the less the movement will be, sometimes this plate is even allowed to protrude past the end of the fixed jaw which is very effective but can be inconvenient, if we are going to make a vice for ourselves this plate creates its own problems in as much as getting a good accurate fit can be

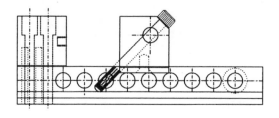
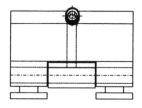
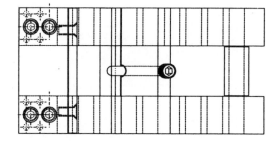

General Arrangement of
the machine vice.

difficult.

This version avoids all these difficulties and in many ways is far easier to construct than the more traditional type, although it can hardly be said that this one is not traditional as the design has been used in tool rooms for at least the last sixty years and yet for some reason is rarely available as a commercial item. Anyway with such an easily made tool who on earth wants to go and buy one? The one shown was made from odd bits that were hanging around in the workshop, providing almost a relief to see some of them at last put to good use. It is quite a small version suitable for drilling, working on a vertical slide, with a milling head attached to the lathe, or perhaps a very small milling machine, in fact it fits very well on a small "Cowell" miller on which fitting other vices of any quality is difficult.

The use of odd bits of material meant that a mixture of Imperial and metric sizes were used, the drawings are given both forms but are not mixed, it is up to the builder to adapt to suit the metal available. The drawings show Imperial and metric measurements suitable to build a vice, these are not necessarily the ones used on the demonstration model. They will work perfectly well but conversion has been such that one or the other only can be used you cannot mix Imperial with metric as they are shown.

Sizes

Up to a point, sizes can be multiplied by any amount to make the size of vice

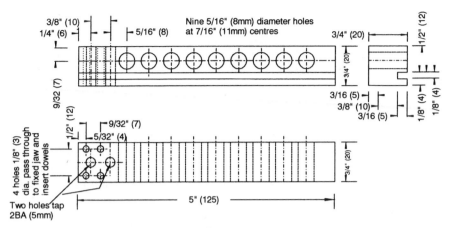

**Base Bars. Two required
left and right handed
from mild steel**

required. Only up to a point because there is one area where adjustments will need to be made when using larger, or indeed smaller material and that is the hole spacing on the base. The distance between the perimeter of the holes should not be more than 3/16" or 5mm otherwise the tilt at the top of the jaw when tightened up might become too exaggerated, they must be correspondingly smaller if a smaller vice is made. That apart, go ahead and do as you please, make a vice to suit a particular job even; it is certainly not a long job and an ideal way of using those odds and ends you don't want to throw away in case they come in handy but have been around the workshop for a number of years.

The Base

The base consists of two lengths of square mild steel bar although rectangular section will do if square is not available, it is simply a case of drilling a series of holes at set centres, ensuring they are square and milling a slot along the length to accept a clamp so that it can be secured to a machine. It is not advisable to use the old trick of clamping the two pieces together and drilling through as the chances of getting it right are pretty slim, almost certainly over a distance like this the drill will wander. In some holes at least if not all. Far better to put the material in the milling vice and use the coordinates on the dials to get the positions right, alternatively this can be done using the vertical slide on the lathe. The holes should be reamed to size if possible although if a suitable reamer is not available there will not be too much harm in drilling them but check the drill is properly ground in order to get the hole as near to size as possible. Four small holes are shown in each piece, which are used for dowels These can be drilled after partial assembly, to ensure they line up accurately with those in the fixed jaw.

Fixed Jaw

The base is held together by the fixed jaw and a spacing bar, or perhaps two spacing bars if you are of a nervous disposition. The fixed jaw should be drilled to accept the Allan Screws that are going to hold it in position and these need to be counterbored to allow the head to be recessed. It will be seen that the clearance holes were put through the top of the jaw and this was because I was not at all certain how things were going to work out, it should be possible to make a far neater job by making the clearance holes and counterbores in the base rather than the way shown and tapping those in the jaw, these can then be blind holes. Before assembling the

It is absolutely essential to check that everything is square as we go along. Here we see the fixed jaw checked with a square at first assembly.

The two jaws:- The fixed one at the rear has been counterbored to accept cap head screws. Some builders may prefer to carry out this operation in the base bars and tap the jaw for the screws. The chamfer can clearly be seen on the moving jaw in the fore-front, together with the clearance hole for the tightening screw.

On the left we can see the plate screwed below the moving jaw to act as a guide between the base bars. The angled hole is also visible and it can be seen that the guide plate has had to be relieved to allow it to protrude.

On the right are the two jaw plates, in this case from mild steel. There is a groove in the one for the fixed jaw to allow round work to be held with safety. It can also be seen how a piece has been filed out to allow the tightening screw to rotate easily. The securing holes are deeply countersunk to clear the heads of the screws that secure the plates.

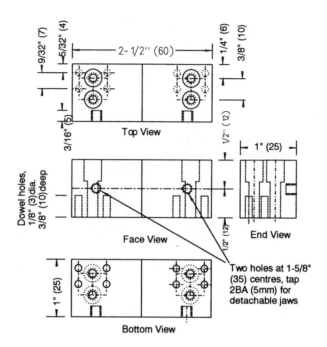

Top View

9/32" (7)

5/32" (4)

2-1/2'' (60)

1/4" (6)

3/8" (10)

3/16" (5)

1/2'' (12)

Dowel holes,
1/8" (3)dia.
3/8" (10)deep

Face View

1/2'' (12)

1" (25)

End View

1" (25)

Bottom View

Two holes at 1-5/8"
(35) centres, tap
2BA (5mm) for
detachable jaws

Fixed Jaw

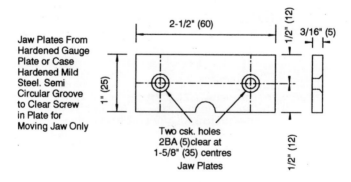

Jaw Plates From
Hardened Gauge
Plate or Case
Hardened Mild
Steel. Semi
Circular Groove
to Clear Screw
in Plate for
Moving Jaw Only

2-1/2" (60)

1/2" (12)

3/16" (5)

1" (25)

1/2" (12)

Two csk. holes
2BA (5)clear at
1-5/8" (35) centres

Jaw Plates

jaw to the base two tapped holes will be needed to accept the removable plates which will act as soft and hard jaws, it is all too easy, to think that it is not necessary to fit these, but in no time at all the actual jaws would become marked and damaged, where as with removable plates they can easily be replaced as and when one wishes.

First Assembly

Once the fixed jaw can be screwed into position fit the spacer, which is made from round stock at the other end, but don't secure it in position, screw on the jaw and check that it is square to the base, if there is any problem tap it with a soft hammer, until it is right. Tighten the screws as hard as they will go and then drill the four dowel holes in each bar of the base, taking each one into the jaw. Check again that everything is square and then slip in pieces of silver steel to act as dowels, after putting a little retaining compound in the hole. Leave it to set and then remove the spacer and bar at the

The finished vice, awaiting the final touches. The holes can be filled with an epoxy resin and after smoothing down with an abrasive paper the surface can be painted.

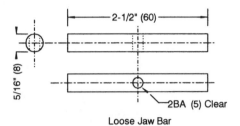

One required, fits in moving jaw. Screw passes through.

2-1/2" (60)

5/16" (8)

2BA (5) Clear

Loose Jaw Bar

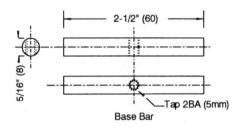

Move to hole in base to suit size of work and screw moving jaw to it.

2-1/2" (60)

5/16" (8)

Tap 2BA (5mm)

Base Bar

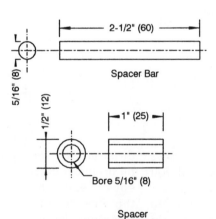

One or two may be used with spacer between base bars, fit assembly with retaining compound.

2-1/2" (60)

5/16" (8)

Spacer Bar

1/2" (12)

1" (25)

Bore 5/16" (8)

Spacer

Bars and Spacer

other end, apply some retainer and reassemble. Make a quick check to ensure everything is right and allow it to set. The base is now complete.

Moving Jaw

The moving jaw is similar to the fixed one but has a chamfer at forty five degrees, which allows the top to move slightly in advance of the bottom. Get the angle as near as possible and then drill through clearance size for the tightening up screw. This will break out at the bottom edge and it is as well to just clean up with a round file where it does so, to ensure that the screw will rotate easily. A locating plate is screwed to the bottom of the jaw just as a guide to fit between the two base bars. Strictly speaking this is not necessary as if the bars used for tightening up are a good fit it will line itself up, but it is better to be safe than sorry.

The removable plates can either be made of mild steel or ground flat stock, otherwise called gauge plate, a lot will depend on the use to which the vice is to be put. A groove with an angle of forty five degrees can be milled in the one for the fixed jaw as an aid to holding round work if you wish, this again is a matter of personal choice. It is worth considering hardening the jaw plates to be used for general work and if gauge plate is used this is straight forward, but if they are mild steel, case hardening will be the only way to do it. The opportunity might also be taken at this stage to make some soft plates of brass or aluminium for use on more delicate work and it is even worth considering plastic ones. The jaw plates will all need to have the tops machined square after fitting but this can be done the first time the vice is put into use. The plates on the moving jaw will need to have a recess filed or milled in them to clear the tightening screw, as shown on the drawings.

Tightening Bars

All that is left to make are the two tightening bars, the one that will fit in the base is cross drilled and tapped, the other cross drilled clearance size, the one in the base is moved along to accept whatever size of metal is in use. If you feel that an even more secure set up is desirable, put another bar and spacer through the hole under the fixed jaw and secure it with retainer. It is not necessary as the vice is rigid enough as it is but it would give a bit of added security and might just be useful to hang some sort of clamp on in an awkward situation. Finally fill up the counterbore holes with an epoxy resin, smooth off and paint the vice. At one time enamel was recommended for such work, now it is possible to get hard wearing acrylic paint as used on motor cars, which is both hard wearing and easy to apply.

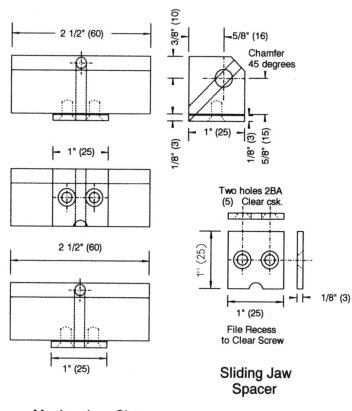

2 1/2" (60)

3/8" (10)

5/8" (16)

Chamfer
45 degrees

1" (25)

1" (25)

1/8" (3)

1/8" (3)

5/8" (15)

2 1/2" (60)

Two holes 2BA
(5)   Clear csk.

1" (25)

1" (25)

1/8" (3)

File Recess
to Clear Screw

**Sliding Jaw
Spacer**

**Moving Jaw, Shown
With Spacer Fitted**